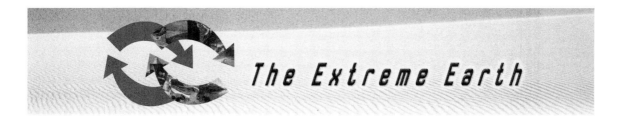

The Extreme Earth

Deserts

Peter Aleshire

Foreword by
Geoffrey H. Nash, Geologist

CHELSEA HOUSE
PUBLISHERS
An imprint of Infobase Publishing

For Elissa, who has been with me for 30 years: not long in geologic time,
but everything in my lifetime

DESERTS

Chelsea House
An imprint of Infobase Publishing
132 West 31st Street
New York NY 10001

Library of Congress Cataloging-in-Publication Data

Aleshire, Peter.
    Deserts / Peter Aleshire.
        p. cm. — (The extreme earth)
    Includes bibliographical references and index.
    ISBN-13: 978-0-8160-6434-2
    ISBN-10: 0-8160-6434-2
    1. Deserts—Juvenile literature. I. Title. II. Series.
    QH88.A44 2008
    551.41'5—dc22   2007008245

Text design by Erika K. Arroyo
Cover design by Dorothy M. Preston/Salvatore Luongo
Illustrations by Melissa Ericksen

Printed in the United States of America

VB FOF 10 9 8 7 6 5 4 3 2 1

This book is printed on acid-free paper.

T 13616

Contents

Foreword

✧✧✧✧✧✧✧✧✧✧✧✧✧✧✧✧✧✧✧✧✧✧✧

If you have ever visited a desert, or seen a movie or documentary set in a desert, you might believe that little, if anything, could exist in such an environment. A visitor to the Mohave Desert of California, for example, may doubt that without regular rainfall, streams, or lakes, anything other than a few well-adapted reptiles could flourish here. After all, we humans would soon perish in an environment devoid of water to drink, not to mention the toll extreme heat would play. Access to water is central to our ability to grow crops and develop industry so deserts may seem forbidding and lifeless to us at first glance. Deserts are extreme environments that are also biologically diverse, and this contradiction makes them interesting to the scientists such as biologists, geologists, and archaeologists who study them. You might think of a desert as a vast expanse of rolling sand dunes, but many consist of a windswept stony pavement, bare bedrock, salt-covered flats, or even ice fields or Arctic tundra. What they share is the basic relationship between rainfall and evaporation. A desert is defined as a region where evaporation exceeds rainfall or, generally, one that receives less than 10 inches (25 cm) of rain per year. Because deserts receive so little rain, geologists are able to study the rocks without a lot of soil or vegetation getting in the way.

In *Deserts*, by Peter Aleshire, you will learn the ways deserts can differ. You will learn about the sustaining sky islands of the Sonoran Desert in Arizona and New Mexico that gather rainwater, allowing wildlife to thrive throughout the seasons as one plant community after another matures at different elevations. Another desert you will read about is the Great Basin Desert in the American Southwest where evaporation over thousands of years since the end of the last ice age caused the formation of the Great Salt Lake and the accumulation of massive amounts of salt and other minerals. Other deserts covered here are the Sahara of northern Africa with the world's tallest sand dunes and the Arabian Desert, home to the perfectly adapted "ship of the desert" or camel.

Deserts are the product of where they are located on Earth because they are produced by climatological factors such as dry winds and rain shadows behind mountains. Because of the movement of continents due to plate tectonics, deserts now exist where forests previously grew and, often, petrified wood has been left behind as proof of the changes caused by climate.

Aleshire's book is an introduction to the study of deserts that will prove useful to a world where many signs point to a process of unprecedented change due to global warming. As areas of Earth are affected by extreme weather patterns, change will come. Additional rainfall may benefit some areas, while loss of regular rain may produce more arid, difficult environments that make life harder for their inhabitants. Readers will find this book an interesting study of some of the most forbidding yet diverse areas on the planet.

—Geoffrey H. Nash, geologist

Preface

✧✧✧✧✧✧✧✧✧✧✧✧✦✧✧✧✧✧✧✧✧✧✧✧✧

From outer space, Earth resembles a fragile blue marble, as revealed in the famous photograph taken by the *Apollo 17* astronauts in December 1972. Eugene Cernan, Ronald Evans, and Jack Schmitt were some 28,000 miles (45,061 km) away when one of them snapped the famous picture that provided the first clear image of the planet from space.

Zoom in closer and the view is quite different. Far beneath the vast seas that give the blue marble its rich hue are soaring mountains and deep ridges. On land, more mountains and canyons come into view, rugged terrain initiated by movement beneath the Earth's crust and then sculpted by wind and water. Arid deserts and hollow caves are here too, existing in counterpoint to coursing rivers, sprawling lakes, and plummeting waterfalls.

The Extreme Earth is a set of eight books that presents the geology of these landforms, with clear explanations of their origins, histories, and structures. Similarities exist, of course, among the many mountains of the world, just as they exist among individual rivers, caves, deserts, canyons, waterfalls, lakes, ocean ridges, and trenches. Some qualify as the biggest, highest, deepest, longest, widest, oldest, or most unusual, and these are the examples singled out in this set. Each book introduces 10 superlative examples, one by one, of the individual landforms, and reveals why these landforms are never static, but always changing. Some of them are internationally known, located in populated areas. Others are in more remote locations and known primarily to people in the region. All of them are worthy of inclusion.

To some people, the ever-shifting contours of the Earth are just so much scenery. Others sit and ponder ocean ridges and undersea trenches, imagining mysteries that they can neither interact with nor examine in person. Some gaze at majestic canyons, rushing waterfalls, or placid lakes, appreciating the scenery from behind a railing, on a path, or aboard a boat. Still others climb mountains, float rivers, explore caves, and cross deserts, interacting directly with nature in a personal way.

Even people with a heightened interest in the scenic wonders of the world do not always understand the complexity of these landforms. The eight books in the Extreme Earth set provide basic information on how individual landforms came to exist and their place in the history of the planet. Here, too, is information on what makes each one unusual, what roles they play in the world today, and, in some cases, who discovered and named them. Each chapter in each volume also includes material on environmental challenges and reports on science in action, with details on field studies conducted at each site. All the books include photographs in color and black-and-white, line drawings, a glossary of scientific terms related to the text, and a listing of resources for more information.

When students who have read the eight books in the Extreme Earth set venture outdoors—whether close to home, on a family vacation, or to distant shores—they will know what they are looking at, how it got there, and what likely will happen next. They will know the stories of how lakes form, how wind and weather work together to etch mountain ranges, and how water carves canyons. These all are thrilling stories—stories that inhabitants of this planet have a responsibility to know.

The primary goal of the Extreme Earth set of books is to inform readers of all ages about the most interesting mountains, rivers, caves, deserts, canyons, waterfalls, lakes, ocean ridges, and trenches in the world. Even as these books serve to increase both understanding of the history of the planet and appreciation for all its landforms, ideally they also will encourage a sense of responsible stewardship for this magnificent blue marble.

Acknowledgments

✧✧✧✧✧✧✧✧✧✧✦✧✧✧✧✧✧✧✧✧✧

I am indebted to the many people who have made this book possible. Geologist Geoffrey Nash provided invaluable technical editing and advice, although any remaining technical imperfections are my fault alone. Agent Jeannie Hanson was the midwife and creator for this whole series and but for her I would not have had the opportunity to write this book. Editor Frank Darmstadt managed to gather up all the bits and pieces for an eight-book series and bring it all together in this form, a wonderful feat of word juggling. I am also grateful for the efforts of assistants Melissa Cullen-DuPont, Alana Braithwaite, and Joyce Smith, who all made this a far better book than I ever could have managed without such wonderful help. Finally, I am grateful to the United States Geological Survey, who provided such generous assistance in helping to find images to illustrate this book.

Introduction

At first look, deserts seem empty—all sky and horizon and aching distance. The plants huddle close to the ground, the creatures hide in burrows and furrows and spidery, dry streambeds. The seasons pass seemingly without measure, with no turning of leaves, no mantling of snow.

But that is all a trick of the eye, like the shimmering mirage of water caused by the heating of the air close to the hot, dry desert surface.

Deserts, another volume in the Extreme Earth set, presents an overview of 10 of the planet's most recent and dynamic desert landscapes. They showcase the fine details of Earth's history—the fractures, layers, and outbursts all laid out in a sweep to the horizon. Deserts yield up clues to life's evolution and shift, from sharks' teeth to dinosaurs' eggs to the fossilized bones of our earliest ancestors. They also demonstrate the startling shifts in Earth's climate, recording both the drifting of continents and the change in weather patterns in their layered fossils, vanished grasslands, and great lakes and seas turned to bizarre salt flats.

The deserts faithfully record the history of the planet, hiding the clues in plain sight in an angular landscape marked lightly by erosion and vivid without a cloying covering of green plants. So fossils and tools left by Stone Age hunters show us that the endless dunes of the vast Sahara were once tree-studded grasslands where hunters with stone-tipped spears stalked great herds. So the flat, hard deserts of Australia harbor the remains of bizarre, giant versions of wombats and kangaroos hunted to extinction just as humans arrived on the island continent and climate shifts turned grasslands to sand flats. So the high, cold, desperately dry deserts in the rain shadow of the towering Andes harbor enigmatic deposits of nitrates that hint at shifting continents and the surprising influence of a great undersea trench just off the coast. So the seeds gathered by pack rats and preserved in their urine-cemented middens in the deserts of New Mexico document the rise of an ancient civilization and the transformation of an oak woodland into a hard, cold desert—perhaps caused by human consumption of vital natural resources. Deserts record both the shifts of climates and the impact of human carelessness.

Deserts also offer a dramatic study of adaptation and change through the history of the people, plants, and animals that live in such harsh environments. So the kangaroo rat of the Sonoran Desert lives its whole life without a drink of water and in its industrious seed-gathering determines the borderline between desert and grassland. So the desert peoples of the Middle East confronted the challenges of the desert and from its austere hardships originated many of the world's great religions. The bushmen of the Australian deserts developed a culture of great dreams and visions, while evolving an ability to nearly shut down their metabolism and wrest a living for more than 20,000 years in a harsh desert with a bare minimum of tools or technology. The camel of the great Middle Eastern deserts developed a miraculous kidney, built-in water storage, feet adapted for sand, and even filters for their eyes and nose to withstand the most severe of sandstorms.

The Hopi Indians who live in the Sonoran Desert of Arizona believe that the first people came into Earth in the middle of that vast and varied desert and then set out across the world to find a good place to live. They found many easy places with lots of rain. But life was so easy in those places that they forgot their prayers. They became greedy and quarrelsome and stopped living in a kind and upright and ethical way. The elders realized then that they must return to the desert, where the heat and winds and long droughts would remind them of the need to be careful and reverential and cooperative. They have lived there ever since, including in a village on a mesa that is now the longest continually occupied settlement in North America. They hold to their prayers there in that great desert, believing that the Creator will destroy the world once again should they flag in their devotion.

Perhaps they are right—at least about the way in which the desert makes human beings value the essential things. Curiously, many of the world's great religions originated among desert peoples and then spread to easier places, where rain is an irritation instead of a blessing.

That alone is reason enough to wish to understand Earth's great deserts.

Origin of the Landform

Deserts

The appearance and evolution of Earth's deserts offer deep insights into geology, history, evolution, climate, and the whole rich history of the planet. Although deserts now cover great swaths of Earth's surface along the broad, hot midsection of the planet, most modern deserts are new landscapes—the transformation of grasslands and woodlands into an austere and revealing terrain that makes special demands of any living creatures who brave it and often thrive.

Although the deserts of North America seem vast in their sprawl across more than 500,000 square miles (1,295 sq km), they're dwarfed by the 3.5 million square miles (7.8 million sq km) of the Sahara Desert, the 1.3 million square miles (3.4 million sq km) of the Australian deserts, or the 1 million square miles (2.6 million sq km) covered by the Arabian deserts.

Generally defined as an area where annual evaporation from the surface exceeds annual rainfall, deserts are the result of a combination of position on the globe, local terrain, and global atmospheric circulation. Most of the deserts of the world lie between 15 and 35 degrees latitude, generally centered over the tropic of Cancer and the tropic of Capricorn. This midsection of the planet receives the most annual sunlight. The energy from the sun heats the air, especially along the equator. This heated air can hold an enormous amount of water. As it rises, much of that water condenses into clouds, which rain down upon the narrow belt of tropical rain forests along the equator, generally about 30 degrees latitude on either side of the equator. Now wrung out, the dry air moves both north and south, cooling as it moves. Eventually, it is cold and heavy enough to descend back down to the surface, creating the dry, wind-prone zones in which most of the Earth's deserts form.

This global circulatory pattern makes most deserts possible, but other factors have to combine to create the perfect conditions for a major desert. As a result, the world's deserts fall into several major types.

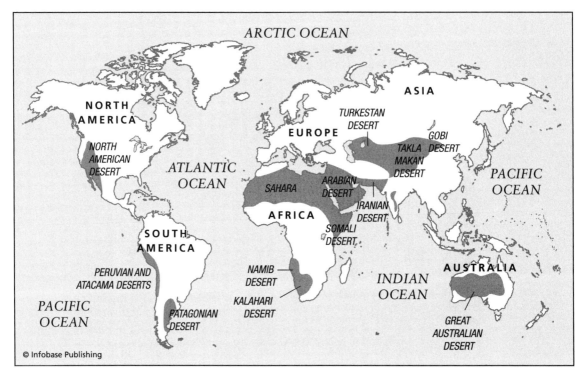

The world's deserts

RAIN SHADOW DESERTS

Many deserts form in low-lying regions that lie in the rain shadow of a major mountain range. Often, such desert-forming mountain ranges lie along coastal regions. When moisture-laden air moves inland off the ocean, it encounters the barrier of the mountains. As the moist air rises to move over the mountain range, it cools so that it can no longer hold all that moisture. The water falls as rain and snow on the mountains so that by the time the air moves into the low-lying regions beyond, it is dry and thirsty. To one degree or another, this rain shadow effect has created all of the deserts of North America.

COASTAL DESERTS

Coastal deserts form on the western edge of continents near the tropic of Cancer and the tropic of Capricorn largely as a result of great currents in the ocean. These great rivers in the ocean move in a great clockwise pattern in the Northern Hemisphere and in a counterclockwise direction in the Southern Hemisphere. Some of those currents start at the poles

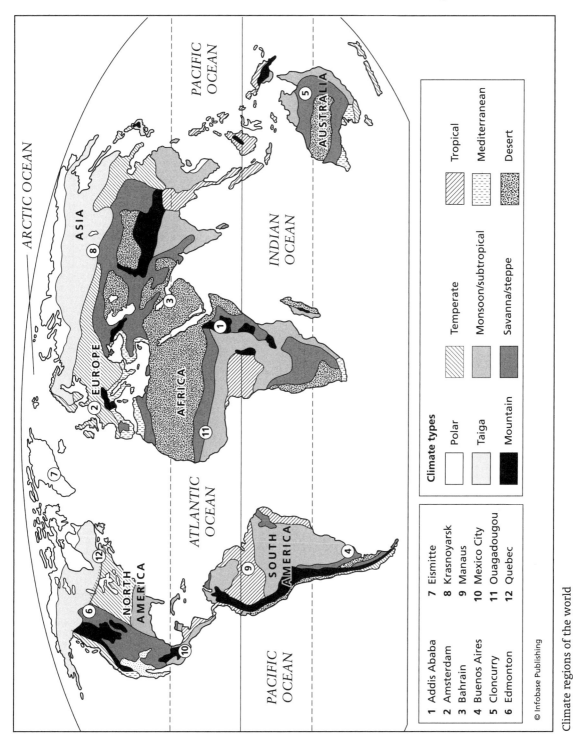

Climate types

☐ Polar	☐ Temperate	▨ Tropical
☐ Taiga	▨ Monsoon/subtropical	⬚ Mediterranean
▨ Mountain	▨ Savanna/steppe	▨ Desert

1 Addis Ababa   7 Eismitte
2 Amsterdam   8 Krasnoyarsk
3 Bahrain   9 Manaus
4 Buenos Aires   10 Mexico City
5 Cloncurry   11 Ouagadougou
6 Edmonton   12 Quebec

© Infobase Publishing

Climate regions of the world

as heavy, chilled water sinks and flows along the western edges of the continents toward the equator. However, on the eastern edge of most of the continents, those currents flow in the opposite direction, moving warm tropical water toward the frigid poles. The cold currents that flow along the west side of most continents do not release water easily to the atmosphere, which means that the coastal areas next to such currents are often starved for water. This helps explain the high, cold, desperately dry deserts of Chile, which lie just opposite the lush rain forests of Brazil.

INTERIOR DESERTS

The final major type of desert forms in remote, interior regions, so far from the ocean that they are cut off from a ready supply of atmospheric water. Water from the warm tropics or the wet oceans that enters the atmosphere drops out as rain long before it reaches these vast interior spaces, which form the harshest deserts on the planet, including the vast Sahara and the Turkestan and Gobi deserts of Asia.

So the locations and dynamics of the world's deserts illuminate vital questions about everything from the positions of the continents to the workings of the climate of the entire planet. For instance, the dramatic increase in the extent of deserts worldwide in recent centuries holds important clues about the impact of human beings on the environment and future shifts in climate.

All of which makes understanding the history, evolution, dynamics, and geology of the deserts essential to understanding the history and fate of both the planet and human beings.

Section I

Deserts of North America

✧✧✧✦✧✧✧

Sonoran Desert

Arizona and Northern Mexico

The towering, bristling, water-hoarding saguaro cactus cluster thickly across the desert corrugations of Saguaro National Monument in Arizona, brooding over a mystery. The defining plant of the Sonoran Desert, the largest of the saguaro are 200 years old, 50 feet high (15.24 m), and weigh eight tons. They dominate the park that occupies two sprawling areas of desert on either side of Tucson.

Countless Hollywood westerns and the efforts of generations of landscape photographers have made the saguaro the icon for the very concept of desert. And this towering plant is perfectly adapted to desert conditions with its backwards photosynthesis, stubborn persistence in the face of drought, and ability to store tons of water gathered after the infrequent but fierce desert rainstorms. In turn, the saguaro supports diverse desert ecology (shown in the color insert on page C-4 [bottom]) and has sustained ancient civilizations. It provides a vital resource for desert birds like the white-winged dove, Gila woodpecker, flicker, and elf owl, not to mention an intricate network of insects, lizards, and bacteria that take full advantage of its rich production of seeds, its sweet fruit, and its ability to store vital moisture through months and then years of drought. Moreover, its surprisingly recent adaptation to desert conditions and spread from its isolated Ice Age sanctuaries throughout northern Mexico and southern Arizona have in the process largely defined the extent of the Sonoran Desert, which remains the most diverse and productive of the world's deserts.

Recent efforts to understand the long, slow, surprisingly vulnerable life span of the saguaro have also shed more light on the complex ecological interactions in a desert where every creature lives on the edge of drought and disaster. The story started years ago when botanists compared photos taken before the establishment of the eastern half of the Saguaro National Monument in 1933 with current photos from the same location. They noted a dramatic decline in the number of young saguaros. Normally, it takes the pleated, green-skinned, shallow-rooted saguaro a decade to grow

Desert kit foxes are shy, nocturnal creatures that can climb trees, scale boulders, hide in burrows, and go for long periods without a drink of water, relying entirely on moisture in the bodies of the mice, kangaroo rats, and insects they consume. *(Peter Aleshire)*

its first inch, half a century to reach 12 feet (3.66 m), and 75 years to sprout branches. Only about one out of the 40 million seeds a saguaro produces in a long lifetime sprouts and produces a saguaro big enough to produce seeds.

Botanists had no idea how to account for the apparent lack of young saguaro in the pictures. Scientists already knew that saguaros germinate in pulses, so that certain wet years produce a bounty crop of sprouts. But they could not find a pattern of wet and dry years that could account for the missing saguaros. Initially, researchers blamed air pollution. They argued that fumes from booming Tucson had stunted the growth of the young saguaros. But that theory also fell apart when careful measurement in the Saguaro National Monument revealed that most of the missing saguaros were the equivalent of teenagers, about 30 to 120 years old.

That insight solved the mystery and revealed the culprits: cattle and woodcutters. Biologists discovered that few saguaro seedlings took root during the period cattle grazed in what became the monument. Although the federal government established the preserve in 1933, park managers didn't exclude cattle until the 1970s. And, when Americans first arrived in Tucson in the late 1800s, woodcutters quickly cut down most of the mesquite, palo verde, and ironwood trees in the park's eastern section. This eliminated the "nurse trees" whose shade and shelter dramatically increase the chance that a young saguaro will sprout and survive its vulnerable first couple of decades. Next, settlers stocked the land with too many cattle, which added to the devastation by chomping on any new nurse tree seedlings and trampling the few saguaro sprouts. The picture became clear after biologists compared the patterns of saguaro growth in the heavily disturbed eastern section of Saguaro National Monument with the quieter western section.

The saguaros, which have also nourished desert-dwelling Native American cultures for millennia, show their long, hard history. Droughts cause drooping, looping arms, birds hollow out nesting cavities, accordion-pleated trunks shrink and swell with the rainfall, frost stunts and warps branches. Through it all, they support a complex ecosystem. The massive trunk of a saguaro is speckled with holes, nest cavities hacked out of the thick, thorned, chlorophyll-containing skin of the saguaro by either Gila woodpeckers or flickers. The saguaro seals the injury with a rush of dopamine, the same substance that produces addiction in the brains of heroine addicts or chocoholics, followed by the output of melanin, which also protects frail, human skin from skin cancer. The mix of sap and chemicals produces a hard, brown "boot," so tough it forms a gourdlike residue in the skeletal remains of a downed saguaro. The woodpeckers occupy their cool, moist nests for a single season, before leaving their digs to a host of other desert refugees, including owls, flycatchers, wrens, martins, starlings, finches, bats, beetles, spiders, and even snakes.

SAGUAROS NOURISH CIVILIZATIONS

Saguaros also sustained desert-dwelling Indians. The Pima and Papago, now called the Tohono O'odham, relied heavily on the sweet, nutritious fruit of the saguaro. They dry-farmed corn, squash, and beans, channeling both winter and summer rains onto farmed terraces and stream meanders. Fortunately, the saguaro fruit offered a nutritional bounty perfectly timed between their twin annual growing seasons. They called the Big Dipper the Cactus Puller for its resemblance to the long, sticks made of the ribs of

The orange and black Gila monster is one of the world's few poisonous lizards and one of the distinctive reptiles of the deserts of the United States and northern Mexico. Slow and rare, the large reptile drips poison into a wound through a groove in its teeth, which it locks onto its prey like a pit bull. However, the slow-moving lizard would rather hide from humans than bite them. The oversized lizard survives hard times and droughts by living off fat supplies in its thick tail. *(Peter Aleshire)*

saguaros they used to knock the succulent red fruits from the saguaros' towering tops.

Some Tohono O'odham stories say the saguaro sprang from beads of sweat dropped into the dust from the brow of one of their deities, I'itoi, who also made human beings. Another story says that a boy neglected by his mother slipped into a tarantula spider hole, to sprout again as the first saguaro. They held the saguaro sacred, burying the placentas of their newborns at the base of one of the sacred trees to invoke long life and lining the graves of their loved ones with saguaro ribs.

The songs of desert Indians express their reverence and respect for the saguaro, like this Papago song translated by Ruth Underhill in *Singing for Power.*

Within itself it rustles as it stands;
Within itself it thunders as it stands;
Within itself it roars as there it stands;
Within it there is much soft rain.

The flowering of the irrepressible saguaro's white, trumpet-shaped flowers in May and June prompted joyful ceremonies. The huge, delicate, luscious flowers generally remain open only for a single night, drawing eager *pollinators.* White-winged doves perch on the crown of thorns by day. True deep-desert birds, white-winged doves fly great distances to water holes and remain one of the few birds that can suck in water, rather than swallowing it a mouthful at a time. The bounty of the saguaro helps them survive the summer. At night, the saguaro nectar sustains long-nose bats, whose migration north out of the Tropics is perfectly timed to take advantage of the flowering of a succession of cacti and agave, including the saguaro. Biologists worry that the sharp decline in the great flocks of migratory, long-nosed bats might pose long-term problems for the saguaro.

Saguaros tower on Sonoran Desert slopes above Phoenix, one of the largest desert cities in history, built at the intersection of three desert rivers that have sustained human beings for more than 10,000 years. Phoenix was named for the mythological bird created from its own ashes because it was built on the ruins of the 1,000-year-old Hohokam civilization. *(Peter Aleshire)*

When the saguaro flowers yield to swollen, lush red fruits, the O'odham scatter across the desert to gather this bounty in the harshest time of the year. Some 600 families would cooperate to gather an estimated 450,000 pounds of saguaro fruit each year. About 25 pounds of fruit could be mashed, strained, and converted into a gallon of thick, reddish-brown syrup that yielded a sweet, mild wine used in ceremonies to invoke blessings and visions and songs. Ruth Underhill, in *Singing for Power*, recorded one Papago song for drinking saguaro wine.

'Tis at the foot of little gray Mountain
I am sitting and getting drunk.
Beautiful songs I shall unfold.

The little playful women,
The little playful women,
Whence got they dizziness?
Therewith they made my heart drunk.
The little playful women,
When they are dizzy
Surely they will take me.

Much dizziness,
Much dizziness
Within me is swelling
And more and more.
Every which way I am falling.

SKY ISLANDS RISE FROM DESERT SEAS

The *basin and range* geography that created all the deserts of North America, in the Sonoran created a chain of 10,000-foot-tall (3,048 m) mountains surrounded by low desert basins that help account for the extraordinary ecological diversity of the Sonoran Desert. One of the most striking mountains is the 7,730-foot-tall (2,356.10 m) Baboquivari in southern Arizona where the Tohono O'odham believe the Creator lives. This sky island provides sanctuary for plants and animals by capturing clouds, gathering rainwater, and providing such diverse habitats that it serves as an ecological island in a desert sea.

Baboquivari also looms in human myth and history, set in the vast Tohono O'odham Indian Reservation along the Arizona/Mexico border, which covers more ground than the state of Connecticut. The Tohono O'odham, whose name means "desert people who have emerged from the Earth," are a quiet, friendly, reverential people with an ancient, but now besieged, cul-

The woody skeleton of a saguaro defines the Sonoran Desert. The giant cactus can live for 300 years and store tons of water in its fleshy, pleated tissues that enable it to survive many months—even years—without rain. Pollinated by bats and white-winged doves, a saguaro produces several million seeds in its lifetime, but often only one or two survive to produce the next generation. *(Peter Aleshire)*

ture. Most of the Baboquivari Mountains remain rugged wilderness, with no roads and only a few trails.

Native American storytellers tell different versions of the creation myth and the role of the peak itself. One story holds that the peak once formed the umbilical cord connecting Heaven and Earth, allowing people and spirits to pass freely back and forth. However, the cord eventually broke, leaving just the stump of its connection in the striking form of Baboquivari Peak. The Tohono O'odham call it *Waw Kiwulik*, which means "rock drawn in at the middle."

Somewhere on the rugged slopes above the trailhead is the cave of I'itoi, who created humans, deer, fire, bald-headed buzzards, and much trouble before retiring into the Earth. Now he grants children good luck, provides medicine men with healing powers, and sends dreams. People still make solemn pilgrimages to the cave, bringing small gifts to leave at the entrance to I'itoi's *labyrinth*. However, the location of the cave remains a secret. In the traditional Tohono O'odham culture, people undertake purifying journeys in the hope that they will be rewarded by a dream that imparts a song with spiritual power. The song will then give them something to offer others, perhaps the power to find lost things or heal snakebites or predict future events or run long distances without tiring. To gain these sacred visions and songs, these desert people would walk 1,000 miles (1,609 km) to the Gulf of California and gather up and return with blocks of salts from the shoreline.

ORGAN PIPE NATIONAL MONUMENT PRESERVES DESERT

On the edge of the Tohono O'odham Reservation stands Organ Pipe National Monument, one of the best places to glimpse the rich *ecosystem* of the Sonoran Desert, with its tenacious, understated extravagance and the long sweep to the horizon. The landscape was forged in a series of cataclysms starting 110 million years ago caused by the bumping and grinding of gigantic crustal plates that shaped the topography of the entire Southwest. The 3,000-foot-high (914 m) Puerto Blanco Mountains are made of 18-million-year-old *rhyolite*, which is really just molten granite spewed out and cooled at the surface instead of deep in the earth. That jagged, unsoftened volcanic history has created an uncompromising landscape, with starkly tormented ridgelines, jagged, gaping canyons, and long rocky slopes.

Deep in the monument burbles Quitobaquito Springs, where a 30-gallon-a-minute spring gushes 2,000-year-old rainwater that runs down a grassy wisp of a stream into a pond. Forced to the surface by a fault that has created an underground dam of crushed rock, the miraculous spring has nourished human beings for millennia. It nurtured desert-dwelling Indians for thousands of years and saved thousands of lives during the California gold

Javelina only resemble Old World wild pigs. In fact, they're a distinct species that have spread out of the deserts of northern Mexico into the Sonoran Desert. Armed with wicked incisors and a fearless disposition, they can kill and eat rattlesnakes, chase off coyotes, happily munch bristling cacti, and have adapted readily to humans. Many people trying to keep gardens on the edge of the desert in cities like Phoenix now have to cope with raids on their flowers by javelina. *(Peter Aleshire)*

rush, when it provided one of the few reliable water sources on the aptly named "Devil's Highway" between Tucson and Yuma.

The Tohono O'odham call the spring *A'al Waipia* (little wells) and farmed it until the government bought them out in 1938 and destroyed one of the oldest human settlements in North America. Now, the pond harbors endangered pupfish, remarkable Ice Age survivors that can tolerate hot, salty, low-oxygen water, but not the excessive pumping of groundwater and the voracious introduced fish that have degraded the streams, ponds, and seeps where it used to live.

The spring has played a vital role in the myths and survival of people stretching back at least 12,000 years, which is the age of finely shaped spear points left by long-vanished mammoth hunters. Although scientists have surveyed less than 3 percent of the monument, they have located more than 400 archaeological sites. When the first Europeans arrived, they found the peaceful and deeply spiritual Tohono O'odham living here, nurtured by a rich culture exquisitely adapted to surviving in a land where it can go a year between rains. They farmed the deep desert, relied on scattered springs and tanks, and regarded the world with reverence and wonder.

The monument also harbors the smoothed and sculpted Sonoyta Mountains, composed of pinkish granite, which cooled deep beneath the surface instead of frothing to the surface like the rhyolite Puerto Blancos. The sunny exposures and cold-air-shedding slopes nurture a surreal wealth of cacti, plus the bizarre elephant tree. A single elephant tree, which thrives

SKY ISLANDS ADD DIVERSITY

The strange rock formations of the Chiricahua National Monument are comprised of fused ash from a cataclysmic volcanic eruption that eroded into fantastic shapes. The Chiricahua Mountains form the boundary between the cold Chihuahuan Desert and the warm, monsoon-blessed Sonoran Desert. *(Peter Aleshire)*

The sky islands scattered throughout the Sonoran Desert help account for its surprising ecological diversity. One such "island" mountain rising from the desert plains is Mount Graham, which rises from the mesquite-studded Sonoran Desert to a height of more than 10,000 feet (3,048 m). This means the peak has conditions more akin to Canada than to the desert at its foot. Mount Graham was built by a 50-million-year-long succession of volcanoes and uplift. During the last Ice Age some 10,000 years ago, mastodons, camels, dire wolves, llamas, short-faced bears, and the humans that hunted them populated the wet southwest region. As the climate warmed, the surviving cold-adapted species were marooned on the mountains and evolved into unique species. Today, Mount Graham and the other sky islands tower over the desert like an ecological ark, hosting five different life zones. The mountain has the highest density of black bears in the Southwest, dozens of different types of trees, hundreds of varieties of birds, and rare creatures like ocelots and perhaps even jaguars.

The mountain bristles with history. Indigenous people have taken advantage of the ability to effectively change seasons by moving up and down the mountain's flanks for at least the last 12,000 years. The Apache arrived shortly before the Spanish in the 1500s and quickly took advantage of the mountain's resources. Apache medicine men still know the secret places to harvest plants needed in their ceremonies and remedies, which is one reason they believe the Mountain Spirits still dwell on the mountain. The U.S. Army then built Fort Graham at the foot of the mountain and a hospital in a flower-graced meadow atop the mountain to provide suffering soldiers respite from the desert heat. Near the foot of the mountain, Billy the Kid killed his first man, a blacksmith who was bullying the slightly built, light-haired teenager.

in Sonora, Mexico, where the bulk of the Sonoran Desert dozes in the sun, perches on a hillside overlooking the road. Squat, thick, strange-leafed, and parchment-barked, the bulbous, otherworldly limbs of the elephant tree have skinlike folds of waxy bark.

The organ pipe and senita cacti that dominate the basin seem no less aesthetic and dramatic. The linear saguaros jostle with the orange-spined, pleated organ pipe and the smooth, gray-bearded senita. More frost-sensitive than the stately saguaro, organ pipe and senita occur together nowhere else in the United States, although they define the Sonoran Desert in Mexico. They have evolved all sorts of adaptations to heat and drought. For instance, their specialized *metabolism* allows them to absorb the sun's energy during the day, but hold their breaths until nightfall when they can open their pores and finish photosynthesis with minimal water loss. They have transformed the leaves they wore in the tropics where they originated into needles, which block up to 80 percent of the sun at their delicate growing tips, protect them from hungry nibblers, and even insulate them against the rare snows.

A BAFFLING MISSING PERSONS CASE

The Sonoran Desert holds the clues to one of history's great missing persons cases, the collapse of distinct but connected 1,000-year-old civilizations throughout the Southwest sometime in the 1400s, just before the arrival of the first Spanish explorers. Human beings have occupied the Sonoran Desert for at least 10,000 years and for perhaps as long as 40,000 years. During the last Ice Age, they hunted mammoths, camels, ground sloths, and other big game across grasslands and oak woodlands. But when the planet's climate shifted at the end of the last Ice Age, the grasslands gave way to desert. A host of desert-adapted plants and animals moved into the new habitat, mostly from dry, hot areas farther south.

Human beings also adapted to the shift from grassland and woodlands to desert. For thousands of years, people wandered across the desert in small bands, taking advantage of the varied resources. The Sonoran Desert benefits from weather patterns that provide reliable winter rains from Pacific storms plus a six-week-long, often-spectacular monsoon rainy season in the summer as a result of storms blowing up from the Gulf of California and the Gulf of Mexico. As a result, small bands could move with the seasons and take advantage of the resources of the sky islands, where they could effectively change the season by changing their elevation.

At some point, these bands of wandering hunters and gatherers discovered agriculture. *Archaeologists* still do not know whether the people of the Sonoran Desert learned how to cultivate corn, beans, and squash on their own or whether they picked up the seeds and the methods from the older and more complex civilizations of Mexico and South America. In any case, the desert people first learned to dry farm (without irrigation ditches or wells) by taking advantage of the twice-a-year rainy season and lack of frequent freezes. Gradually, between 1,000 and 1,500 years ago, they started building irrigation works to water crops on the floodplains of the great desert rivers of the Sonora, like the Colorado, Gila, Verde, and Salt. These rivers each drain thousands of square miles of mountainous terrain, which means that the low deserts through which they ran could support much more diverse and numerous cultures than virtually any other desert in the world.

These people built a bewilderment of complex, innovative, exquisitely adapted civilizations throughout the Southwest, mostly based on farming and supplemented by hunting and gathering up wild foods like saguaro fruit and the bean pods of mesquite. They included the *Ancestral Puebloans*, or Ancient Pueblo People, often referred to as the Anasazi, in the North, the Hohokam in central Arizona, and a host of other related people, like the Sinagua, Mogollon, Salado, and others. They established trading networks that exchanged shells from the coast of California for turquoise dug up from the hills of New Mexico and parrots captured in the jungles of Mexico. But after thriving despite droughts and floods and the vagaries of the desert for 1,000 years, all these desert cultures first converted their sprawling villages and cities into fortresslike cliff dwellings and then abandoned even them.

One major archaeological dig attempting to figure out what happened to these ancient civilizations took place on the shores of the Salt River, one of the most important rivers in the Sonoran Desert. Archaeologists unearthed huge villages built 800 years ago along the riverbanks on the edge of what had become a reservoir providing drinking water and flood control for Phoenix, some 100 miles to the west.

Here, the Salado people built huge platform mounds: a set of mud and stone rooms built atop an earlier, filled-in structure from which a growing elite could survey their domain. A network of these mounds was constructed by the Salado people in the cradle of the Tonto Basin, where they thrived for perhaps 500 years thanks to miles of irrigation canals that enabled them to water thousands of acres of farmland. But they disappeared along with all the other desert civilizations some 600 years ago. The dig uncovered pot shards, tumbled walls, ancient bones, and enigmatic figurines and unearthed an ancient observatory, all of which helped provide clues to the mystery.

The dig was triggered by a $347-million project to raise the height of Roosevelt Lake dam. That project was triggered by studies of ancient tree rings showing that the dam could be hit by floods four times the size of any on record. Until researchers put together thousands of tree-ring growth patterns from ancient living trees, downed logs, and the logs cut for roof beams in 1,000-year-old ruins, no one had any idea about the flood danger. Trees put on a thick growth ring in wet years and a thin one in dry years, which means the growth rings over a large area indicate rainfall patterns going back for nearly 2,000 years. The analysis demonstrated that the Sonoran Desert could suffer far greater floods than anyone suspected based on the records of the past century or two. Moreover, the tree-ring data proved that the Sonoran Desert could also go through droughts lasting for 30 years or more. Those discoveries made the 1,000-year survival of the Salado civilization all the more impressive.

The Tonto Basin dig uncovered several long, oversized rooms that were dominated by massive mud and stone columns, pillars that once held beams to support high ceilings. Yet no one lived in the enigmatic structure, as evidenced by the lack of cooking hearths and household debris. Archaeologist David Jacobs, a medic in Vietnam who had been estranged from his own time and culture ever since, managed to solve the mystery of these mysterious structures. Smallish, bearded, supple, and weathered as richly worn leather, Jacobs sometimes rode with the Hells Angels between digs. He discovered that the huge, unoccupied rooms were used as solar observatories, since the doorways and pillars were oriented so that light would stream through the door and reach an alcove on the opposite wall only at dawn on summer solstice, the longest day of the year. This enabled the Salado to calibrate both their ceremonies and harvest.

The platform mounds turned out to be the key to reconstructing the Salado civilization. The pillar site was the oldest mound: a ceremonial center built about A.D. 1000 oriented toward the sun and forming the focal point of a loose alliance of mostly independent farmers and gatherers. But nearby platform mounds built some 200 years later presented a very different picture. The largest, dubbed schoolhouse mound, constituted a bustling, L-shaped assemblage of about 115 rooms that served as an economic center dominating huge tracts of surrounding farmland. Some 200 people lived on the mound, guarding granaries crammed with enough surplus food to last for years. Such a center marked the beginnings of a complex, stratified society. The big cities with platform mounds alongside the irrigation canals housed the priests and the elites. Meanwhile, a network of connected rural settlements housed extended families who were loosely associated with the platform mounds and who harvested the wild resources of the Sonoran Desert, including prickly pear, cholla, agave, and saguaro fruit.

Arizona State University archaeologist Glen Rice, a mild-mannered man with a boyish shock of hair, a neatly trimmed beard, and an air of dogged obsession, sold the Bureau of Reclamation on a project of nearly unprecedented scope. Bespectacled and intense, Rice is an archaeologist of the new school: He loves computers and designed a project in which every artifact has been logged into a computer, including more than 123,000 fragments of pots and 44,000 stone tools. Machines that analyze the trace elements in bones provided clues to diets, including everything from meat content to water sources. Chemical analysis of pot shards even revealed the source of the clays and pigments and helped reconstruct trade networks linking the Salado to other cultures stretching from Mexico to Colorado. Machines that measured different types of carbon dated wood samples, enabling scientists to construct a chronology from bits of charcoal in ancient hearths. Chemical analysis of things like obsidian and turquoise pinpointed sources of precious minerals and so helped reconstruct trade networks. Microscopic analysis of pollen grains and other plant remains helped reconstruct ancient diets, gauging the relative importance of irrigated crops and wild foods. Tree-ring analysis allowed the researchers to reconstruct stream flow year by year.

Gathering such evidence requires hundreds of hours spent shifting dirt through screens and digging with dental tools to find delicate artifacts. An archaeological dig in progress simmers with slow-motion excitement. Someone might find the intact rim of a gigantic storage pot, triggering happy shouts. Then the painstaking excavation continues for hours, or days, as the treasure emerges, inch by inch.

The people who do the dirty work are a varied bunch of scientific vagabonds. Most have degrees in archaeology and constantly move around the country. Most read voraciously, think nothing of a 500-mile (805 km) weekend drive to visit another dig, and have sacrificed marriages, money, and a normal suburban lifestyle to search for the past on hands and knees on some remote, sun-seared slope. Some, like Jacobs, remain quietly out of place, ironic, relentlessly curious, vibrating with life and its possibilities, but tinged with an ancient skepticism. They are discovery junkies, hooked on the thrill of discarded mysteries and the rush of insight. They treasure the moments of contact with a vanished culture. ASU's Glen Rice recalls the day he found a perfect palm print on one of those enigmatic pillars. "There was a Salado hand looking at you, from 900 years ago. That is the thing that is quasimystical. We are not just studying pots and mud and stuff."

A LONG BUILDUP AND A FAST COLLAPSE

The earliest settlers in the Tonto Basin were most likely migrants from the Hohokam core areas in what are now Phoenix and Tucson, where tens of thousands of people tended hundreds of miles of irrigation canals. But they soon evolved their own vibrant culture. They made beautiful pots, painted with elegant, curved designs suggestive of bird wings and sunbursts, that were traded or emulated across the Southwest. They built great food storehouses, reaping the bounty of a frost-free climate that offered rich wild plant resources plus three plantings a year. They buried their dead reverently, along with possessions treasured in life, usually close by their settlements. In one touching case of professional pride, archaeologists unearthed the simple burial of a man interred with his potter's tools and a lump of unworked clay. Often, the Salado buried their babies in the floors of their houses, as though the family sought to protect the spirit of someone too young to have mastered death alone.

Clearly, Salado society grew increasingly complex and stratified as they farmed 44 miles (70.8 km) of streambed. Many lines of evidence converge: the shift from largely ceremonial platform mounds to bustling food store-houses; the first signs of upper-class houses atop the mounds; the concentration of weapons and precious resources like turquoise at the later mounds; an increasing shift to reliance on irrigated crops; the emergence of specialists, like potters.

Then, however, their complex civilization collapsed in a matter of decades. Strangely, no major shifts in the stream coincided with the abandonment, which rules out flood or drought that destroyed the irrigation systems. The 1400s also brought no record-breaking droughts, according to tree-ring studies. Small droughts came and went, but that is not unusual in a watershed where the runoff varies each year from 2.6 million to 162,000 acre feet (enough water to cover one acre to a depth of one foot). The Salado weathered many such droughts during the centuries of their occupation of the valley.

Unfortunately, firm answers must wait on years of analysis as the scientists try to assemble clues to this absorbing missing persons case. "I still don't know why I was drafted in '68, and I'll never know why the Salado disappeared, but I can make good guesses about them both," noted Jacobs. "I'm always trying to get into their position, but I don't even have an appreciation for what would have been a comfortable day's walk. Most Americans know when Easter is, but they don't know it's the first Sunday after the first full moon after the vernal equinox. Americans have no appreciation for what goes on out there at the horizon and where the stars go. I'm sure the people who lived out here 1,000 years ago knew all about that."

At the moment, the evidence suggests the Salado were overtaken by a disaster of their own making, which offers a cautionary tale for modern societies. Perhaps they grew so numerous and so dependent on irrigated crops that a drought they once would have withstood did them in because they had denuded the wild resources of the basin. Perhaps they were affected by the collapse of the Hohokam civilization to the west, epidemics, or warfare with both one another and outside groups that caused their civilization to become more divided and class conscious.

Already, archaeologists have found one tantalizing suggestion that warfare played a tragic role in Salado society. The story emerged fitfully as the archaeologists shifted through centuries of dirt. First they found burned roof beams lying in disorder on the floor. Then they found an arrow point, embedded in what had been a doorway. Finally, trapped beneath the burned roof beams, they found three skeletons, lying facedown on what had been the floor of their home. Evidently, their settlement had been raided. The waist-high compound walls would have provided little protection from determined attackers. They had taken refuge in their home, only to have it set afire. They died there, testament to the persistence of human striving and malice.

MORE CLUES IN THE VERDE VALLEY

More clues to the mystery have been unearthed 100 miles (160.9 km) northwest in the Verde Valley, which harbors some well-preserved ruins constructed by the cliff-house–dwelling Sinagua, who also abandoned an ancient and adaptable Sonoran Desert civilization in the 1400s, including well-constructed stone pueblos at Tuzigoot, Montezuma Castle, and Montezuma Well.

The mysterious Sinagua settlement of Tuzigoot sits alongside the Verde River and represents the climax of a human occupation of the Verde Valley stretching back perhaps 10,000 years to Ice Age mammoth hunters. The Sinagua came after these big game hunters vanished and began farming along the Verde River between A.D. 1 and 700.

The Sinagua built large villages and nourished trade routes stretching from New Mexico to California and from Colorado deep into Mexico, including the Hohokam to the south and the Ancestral Puebloans to the north. Initially, the Hohokam exercised the greatest influence and the Sinagua built Hohokam-style ballcourts and platform mounds. As the tide shifted in favor of the Puebloans, the Sinagua built cliff-houses, imported their ceramics, and buried their dead with an array of prized possessions.

Tuzigoot marks the peak of the Sinagua civilization in the 1300s when thousands of people lived in 50 large pueblos scattered along the Verde River. Set on a rounded hill, the 100-room settlement built between 1125 and 1400 commanded both a loop of the Verde River and the spring-fed Tavasci Marsh. Archaeologists unearthed a Mexican macaw buried carefully in the floor; a medicine man's bag containing a bone whistle, carved fetish, obsidian point, and quartz crystal; a 3,295-bead necklace adorning a "magician's" neck; exquisite inlaid turquoise jewelry; gemstones; a little boy buried with his juniper wood bow; a mother buried with her six-year-old child; and the graves of hundreds of infants laid lovingly to rest in the floors of their parents' apartments. Archaeologists speculate that these in-home burials ensured that the mothers' spirits could eventually lead the children on into the next world.

Nearby stands the beautifully constructed five-story, 20-room Montezuma Castle, perched beneath an overhang in a limestone cliff overlooking Wet Beaver Creek. Together with a now mostly vanished 45-room pueblo, Montezuma Castle sheltered up to 300 people and was accessible only through long ladders.

Several miles up the creek stands yet another Sinagua ruin, set into the crater of Montezuma Well. The well formed when a gigantic limestone cavern created by an underground hot spring collapsed, leaving a crater in a hill. Nearby Beaver Creek cut an outlet at the well's base, and the 1,000-gallon-per-minute spring at the bottom of the 55-foot-deep (16.8 m) well thereafter maintained a constant water level. The valley's earliest inhabitants discovered the well and used the outlet to provide a steady supply of irrigation water. Native American legends hold that our world, the Fourth World, started here long ago. Human beings fled the first three worlds just ahead of rising floodwaters caused by gods disgusted with human strife, greed, and deceit. Human beings wiggled through this hole in the roof of the Third World, and the floodwaters rose into the well and then halted.

CASA MALPAIS: DEATH BY RELIGIOUS WARFARE?

One of the most intriguing clues to the mystery of the regional collapse of ancient civilizations throughout the Southwest lies on a high plateau grassland that lies at the edge of both the Sonoran and Great Basin deserts—the stone ruins of Casa Malpais, a 50-room pueblo on a lava flow riddled with caves. Casa Malpais is the most visible and accessible of a string of pueblos built along the headwaters of the Little Colorado River, which runs down through the Painted Desert, a subdivision of the Great Basin Desert, and on down into the Grand Canyon, which harbors a threadlike piece of the Mojave Desert.

The ruins dream in the sun: great wooden beams hauled by hand for 20 miles (32.2 km); a huge kiva (ceremonial structure) linked to the spirit world; windows and slots that allow summer solstice light to fall on intricate pictoglyphs; a network of exquisitely engineered irrigation canals. But these ruins harbor even deeper secrets—beneath lie the only known *catacombs* in the prehistoric West. And in the architecture and artifacts, these ruins along the Little Colorado also hold clues about the birth of a new religion that may help account for the collapse of civilizations throughout the Southwest.

The village once supported 200 to 400 people and includes many pictoglyphs and astronomical sites. One platform apparently provided a place to tether a captive eagle for ceremonies, since many Pueblo people considered eagles to be divine messengers passing between Heaven and Earth. The village was built in the late 1200s and largely abandoned by the late 1300s, including an observatory designed so that the rising sun would illuminate designs on the walls on the longest and shortest days of the year. The designs on the walls include a flying parrot, a double spiral that suggests an emerging corn sprout, a woman the Zuñi say represents a sacred corn maiden, a bear paw, symbols for migration, the sun, and ancestral beings.

The discovery of catacombs below Casa Malpais caused an archaeological sensation. Both the Hopi and the Zuñi objected to disturbing the bodies of people they consider their ancestors. So the city of Springerville agreed to seal the catacombs, with suitable prayers and offerings by Hopi and Zuñi spiritual leaders.

The waters and springs that feed the Little Colorado originate in the surrounding mountains. The river wanders across the 7,000-foot-high (2,133 m) volcanic plateau and on down through grasslands and deserts to the Grand Canyon. The stretch of slow, muddy river water between St. Johns and Springerville offers one of the few areas where ancient people could divert water to irrigate farmland. As a result, the region has lured people for thousands of years. The irrigation-based civilization that arose here between about A.D. 1000 and 1400 was influenced by surrounding groups and may have welcomed migrating groups from different areas. This blending of cultures spurred the development of the kachina religion, which then spread throughout the Southwest. The rise of the kachina religion may have led to the decline of the dominant religion centered in Chaco Canyon in New Mexico, the high point of the Anasazi (Ancestral Puebloan) civilization. This may help explain the decline of the highly centralized Chaco culture, with its baffling system of wonderfully engineered roads made by a people with no horses or cattle and therefore no use for the wheel.

Casa Malpais and the nearby ruins may have played a crucial role in this transformation due to their uniquely documented mingling of different cultures. In addition, the region forms the overlapping frontier dividing two of the oldest and most vital of the pueblo cultures, the Zuñi and the Hopi.

The Zuñi, linguistically related to groups in California, believe they emerged from a previous world in the depths of the Grand Canyon. They then followed the Little Colorado River out of the Grand Canyon and across the desert to their homeland on a cluster of windswept mesas in New Mexico. For centuries, they have maintained shrines in the area. Religious leaders make regular pilgrimages to these sites within view of the surrounding sacred mountain peaks. They pray and leave tokens in some of the caves, whose locations remain secret. They say the Little Colorado is the umbilical cord that connects them to their origins and call the place where the rivers meet near Casa Malpais "Zuñi Heaven."

The Hopi, linguistically related to the Aztecs in Mexico, believe they also emerged from a previous world drowned by the Creator because of the foolishness and wickedness of human beings. The different clans set out on epic migrations, seeking the best place to live. They explored the world and found many lush places. But finally all circled back to the Hopi mesas, realizing they would lose their way spiritually in such easy places. They realized the harshness of their homeland would hold them to their prayers and right thinking. Their oral traditions hold that several clans came to the Hopi mesas from the area around Casa Malpais, including the Kangaroo Rat, Turkey, Road Runner, Boomerang, Fire, Stick, Butterfly, Bamboo, Reed,

Greasewood, Coyote, Hawk, Spider, and Parrot Clans. They call the area around Casa Malpais *Wenima* and say that the kachinas lived here, which reinforces the evidence of pottery shards and pictoglyphs.

The rich Zuñi and Hopi oral traditions, plus recent archaeological findings, suggest that this stretch of river with its 10 known villages is crucial to understanding the dynamic mingling of cultures and ideas that shaped the prehistory of the region and perhaps help explain the mysterious collapse of farming-based, pueblo-building cultures throughout the Southwest. The evidence shows that over a period of several hundred years these settlements along the Little Colorado River provided a cultural melting pot, taking ideas from all the nearby cultures and blending them into something new.

This has prompted some archaeologists to argue that the kachina religion emerged from this cultural cross-fertilization. This new religion would have challenged the centralized theology of Chaco, which made possible the huge settlements, massive irrigation works, and expertly cobbled roads radiating outward from Chaco for hundreds of miles. That highly centralized Chaco system may have faced a crisis, which the prayers of the Chaco-oriented priests failed to avert. That would have spurred the spread of the kachina religion, which was connected to older traditions. The decline of Chaco coincides with the spread outward from the Casa Malpais area of kachina motifs on pottery found in villages and burials. Moreover, the rise of the decentralized kachina religion coincides with the decline of centralized, irrigation-based civilizations throughout the Southwest.

This absorbing history of triumph and collapse of desert civilizations over the course of 1,000 years illustrates both the bounty and the dangers in even the richest of the world's deserts. This jagged, often-harsh landscape has also spawned an equally vivid and fascinating recent history, including the most compelling myths and stories of the fabled American West.

SUPERSTITION MOUNTAINS AND THE LEGEND OF THE LOST DUTCHMAN

The jagged Superstition Mountains just outside of Phoenix show another face of the Sonoran Desert, rife with alluring legends of violent death and lost gold mines. That includes one of the most famous tales of the Sonoran Desert, the lost gold mine of the mysterious, semi-mythological Jacob Waltz, better known as the "Lost Dutchman."

The German-born Waltz wandered into the area in the 1870s, when Apaches still haunted the rugged canyons and desperate prospectors dreamed of giant gold nuggets. His mysterious life has since been encrusted with myth, like a vein of gold-laced quartz gleaming in a bed of lava. He worked for a time in the rich Vulture mine in Wickenburg before wandering into the Apache-haunted Superstitions.

Supposedly, decades before early Spanish settlers discovered gold in the Superstitions on their sprawling land grant. However, Apaches repeatedly killed first the Spanish and then the Mexican explorers, ranchers, and gold seekers who wandered into that sharp-edged landscape of dead volcanoes, looming lava flows, bizarre *hoodoos* of fused volcanic ash, and boot-piercing scatterings of cholla. No documents have emerged to back up the tales of a mine deep in the contorted heart or the supposed 1848 Apache ambush of a party loaded with gold.

The Apaches wandered freely through the Superstitions and took a dim view of prospectors, believing that digging in the Earth for gold was profane.

Today, the Superstitions are a federally protected wilderness area that showcases the Sonoran Desert. During moderately wet years, the front slope of the Superstition Mountains erupts into a sea of yellow as the desert brittlebushes burst into flower in the spring. About once every eight years, an exceptionally wet winter makes the desert slopes shimmer with seas of Mexican poppies, intermingled with lurid purple outbursts of owl's clover and other wildflowers. The outburst of color transforms the harsh desert into a fantasy world stolen from *The Wizard of Oz*.

FLOWERS BLOSSOM IN THE DESERT

The hardy desert wildflower seeds can lie, desiccated and dreaming in the desert soil for decades, waiting for the steady winter rains they need to flourish in the spring. They are testament to the gaudy persistency of life, especially flowering plants, which emerged approximately 140 million years ago. As leaves evolved into petals loaded with pollen, flowering plants enlisted both insects and the wind to spur their reproduction. This enabled them to spread out of the swamps and shorelines across the continents, occupying every ecological niche and cranny. Flowering plants have now developed some 250,000 species. Flowering grasses spread across the land, supporting all the grazing animals and farmers.

Recent studies have demonstrated that this extravagant display of flowers actually helps maintain the boundaries of the desert. Desert wildflowers only stage their fitful riot of color in wet years, remaining coiled up in seed form for decades at a time. During such wet years, flowers blossom in such abundance that they soak up every excess drop of rain. As a result, even during wet years in the desert, virtually none of the rain that falls to the desert soil makes it past the root zone of the beautiful but thirsty flowering annuals. As a result, the flowers that seem too fragile to survive at all in the desert actually help to maintain the desert, using the water that might otherwise get into the shallow water table to sustain other plants and grasses.

That makes the Superstition's extravagant display of wildflowers all the more significant, especially the frail, moist, paper-thin petals of the poppies.

Poppies come in several hundred varieties. They grow in a cluster of flowers swaying on long stems from a single plant, a pattern called inflorescence, a treasure of a word. One sort of Asian poppy incubates its unripened seeds in a milky sap, which can be turned into opium. The potent chemicals the poppies use to deter the wrong sorts of insects may also cause epidemics of fatal dropsy and blindness in places like India where poppy seed oil is used in cooking. Poppies are also used to make artists' paints, soap, and cake.

Despite their seemingly frail beauty, the seeds of poppies, lupines, and others can lie undaunted in a mere rumor of topsoil, surviving blazing summers, seed-collecting ants, and a decade of drought, yearning for just the right moment. They can cling to life's secret for an astonishing span of time.

THE LETHAL SECRET OF THE LOST DUTCHMAN

When Jacob Waltz and his partner Jacob Weiser emerged from the Superstition Mountains with a handful of gold nuggets, people naturally assumed they had discovered gold in the unlikely geology of the volcanic Superstition Mountains. And when Waltz one day emerged from the mountains without his partner who he said had been killed by the Apache, many people assumed Waltz had murdered his sidekick to keep the gold for himself.

In fact, gold and silver usually form at great depths and pressure in formations that include granite and quartz, so the still raw volcanic formation of the Superstition Mountains in the heart of the Sonoran Desert was an unlikely place for a gold mine. Some now argue that Waltz stole nuggets from the Vulture Mine when he worked there and then passed them off as the gleanings from his mysterious mine. In any case, Waltz never brought in more than a dribble of gold. As his health dwindled, he moved to Phoenix. He died in 1891, nearly penniless. On his deathbed, he solidified his legend by telling his neighbor that he had discovered a rich vein of gold in the shadow of Weaver's Needle, an awesome volcanic plug in the heart of the Superstitions. Before he died, the Dutchman drew a vague map and left it with his neighbor Julia Thomas.

People have been seeking the Dutchman's probably nonexistent mine ever since. In the 1930s, the elderly Dr. Adolph Ruth arrived in Apache Junction, clutching what he said was a copy of Waltz's deathbed map. He set off into the Superstitions on a sweltering summer day and vanished. His skull, perhaps with a bullet hole, turned up several months later. Treasure hunters set out periodically in the ensuing decades. Several died lonely deaths from exposure, cave-ins, or undetermined causes. The gold fever peaked in the 1950s, when two groups of prospectors camped in the shadow of Weaver's Needle and started a shooting war. Three died before a truce was declared. The search for buried gold has settled down since, spawning daydreams, occasional forays, and a wealth of books and articles, without a trace of ore.

The 15,000-year-old seeds of Arctic lupine have been culled from frozen tundra and coaxed into germination. The Mexican poppy seeds produced on the flanks of Superstitions may lie inert for decades, awaiting the perfect, still mysterious combination of sun and rain that produces an explosion of color.

BUENOS AIRES: THE GRASSLAND BOUNDARY

The Sonoran Desert remains a surprisingly fragile ecosystem and has repeatedly shifted its boundaries in response to climate changes and other influences. In wet periods, grasslands expand into desert regions. During droughts and climate shifts, the grasslands retreat and the desert expands. Even insects and animals can affect the boundary between desert and grassland. Creatures whose presence can determine the boundary between two distinct habitats are called *keystone species*. For instance, kangaroo rats are so efficient at gathering up seeds and so well adapted to desert conditions that their industrious seed-gathering determines the boundary between grassland and desert. Harvester ants, which gather up huge quantities of seed, have a similar impact.

Human beings remain the most dramatic of the keystone species, since their activities have a huge impact on ecosystems and now even the climatic patterns of the entire planet. One of the best places to glimpse the impact of human beings on deserts and grasslands and the boundary between them lies in southern Arizona near the border with Mexico where a nature preserve protects a frail fragment of grasslands that once covered much of southeastern Arizona, but which now has largely become the Sonoran Desert.

The grass-graced Buenos Aires Wildlife Refuge, just 60 miles from Tucson, was established to salvage the masked bobwhite quail, pronghorn antelope, and a host of other grassland-dependent species. This refuge is nearly all that remains of a once sprawling grassland ecosystem that was consumed by a century of intense grazing, invading grasses, and smothered wildfires. The refuge lies in the long shadow of Baboquivari, which the Tohono O'odham believe forms the broken umbilical cord between Heaven and Earth where they believe the Creator, I'itoi, still lives. The refuge now harbors pronghorns, four sorts of quail, and a species count that includes 320 birds, 58 mammals, 42 reptiles, 11 amphibians, and more than 600 plants.

The plight of the once-common masked bobwhite quail demonstrates the human impact on the environment. The bobwhite, a droll, brick-red flurry of feathers in the waving, poppy-spattered grass, still holds out in portions of the Sonoran Desert in Mexico and on the Buenos Aires refuge. Keeping them company are the pronghorns, which the Apaches called "One

Who Is Becoming" because its ghost face and unearthly speed made it seem part spirit, part animal.

The refuge runs up the Altar Valley, where giant ground sloths, camels, huge bison, horses, monster beavers, mammoths, and saber-toothed tigers wandered during the last Ice Age. Prehistoric hunters and then the Hohokam left their traces in the valley. The Apache arrived in the 1500s and 1600s to hunt the antelope, driving the farming-based Tohono O'odham back toward the fastness of Baboquivari.

Once the army subdued the Apache, the number of cattle in the southeastern grasslands rose from around 5,000 in 1870 to 1.5 million in 1990. Periodic droughts prompted the starving cattle to eat everything in sight, dramatically altering the grasslands. Droughts in the 1890s, 1920s, and 1950s left piles of cattle bones and converted most areas of the rolling grasslands into mesquite-dominated desert. Instead of a broad, grass-nourishing flow across the valley, storms scoured out a 20-foot-deep (6.9 m), 1,400-foot-wide (426.7 m), 40-mile-long (64.4 km) *arroyo* down the middle of the valley.

In the past 18 years in the refuge, the exclusion of cattle and the restoration of grassfires have dramatically increased native grasses, slowed erosion, and boosted key grassland species. However, the efforts to bring back both the pronghorn and the bobwhite quail illustrate the difficulty of putting Humpty Dumpty back together.

The refuge remains the only place in North America where four species of quail live, including Gambel's, scaled, Montezuma, and masked bobwhite. The masked bobwhite remains the most heavily dependent on thick, continuous grasslands for its survival, perhaps because it eats smaller seeds, feeds its young exclusively on summer grasshoppers, and relies on freezing into invisibility in the deep grass when threatened.

Despite the return of the grassland, the reintroduced bobwhites still struggle for lack of survival skills, since they do not have wild-smart parents to teach them how to survive sudden storms, sporadic freezes, intermittent droughts, hungry coyotes, patrolling hawks, and slithering snakes. Although the refuge's captive breeding program has released 22,000 captive-bred birds, the refuge's bobwhite population hovers at only 200 to 300 and has been dwindling in the face of the ongoing drought. Quail captured in Mexico and released on the refuge do better than the captive-reared birds, but overgrazing and drought in Mexico have nearly wiped out the wild populations there too.

Efforts to reintroduce the pronghorn have also struggled. Ice Age survivors, the pronghorns rely on binocular vision and spectacular speed. With enormous eyes that give them vision equal to binoculars with a wide field of vision, pronghorn can spot an approaching threat from four miles off. They can run for long distances at 40 miles an hour and sprint at 60 miles per hour by taking 27-foot (8-m) strides and landing on exquisitely evolved pads of cartilage. They burn oxygen three times as fast as most animals, thanks to a huge heart and a windpipe more than twice as big as a human's. Although they resemble African antelope, they are actually their own separate species, with feet like a goat and unique pronged horns that shed their sheath each year.

They thrived for 40 million years before Europeans arrived. But long-range rifles enabled hunters to slaughter them by the wagonload. At one point in the late 1800s, hunters sold miners four pronghorns for a quarter. A population estimated in the tens of millions plunged to 30,000 in 1920, including 650 in Arizona. Fortunately, nationwide conservation efforts have boosted the population back to 1 million pronghorn nationally and 60 at Buenos Aires.

GILA RIVER: PLIGHT OF THE DESERT

Nothing so captures the human impact on the Sonoran Desert as the plight of the Gila River, once its most important river system. The river has all but vanished into reservoirs, irrigation ditches, and thickets of exotic salt cedar along most of its once epic length. The ghost river originates in the highlands of New Mexico and runs down to join the Colorado River at Yuma and has played a vital role in the history of the American West. Along this river armies, gold seekers, Indian fighters, and explorers all struggled. Here also a brave but reckless family met its fate in a massacre that shocked the nation.

The river returns only fitfully, when winter floods fill Painted Rock Reservoir, built mostly to prevent floods from ripping through farmland near Yuma. Serious flooding in 1993 washed out great swaths of farmland, provoking an ongoing debate about whether taxpayers ought to pay for the flood works necessary to reclaim the farmland, especially since the series of channels and dikes would doom the patches of cottonwoods and willows that have sprouted after the '93 floods. Dense galleries of cottonwoods and willows once lined many desert streams and rivers in the Sonoran Desert, but woodcutters, dams, diversions, dropping water tables, and the invasion of other trees like the salt cedar have devastated most of the cottonwood-willow habitat, which biologists say are the most biologically productive habitat type outside of the rain forests. Now only during flood does the Gila rise with a liquid gurgle from its dusty tomb and flow unhindered to the Colorado once again.

Desert rivers like the Gila and the Colorado have long offered a lush living to millions of migrating birds. Early accounts indicate that the meandering course of the Gila was marked by groves of cottonwoods and dense thickets of willow, both of which seed readily and grow like weeds on wet sandbars. The river meandered along this gentle incline, hedged by tangled mesquite bosques (forests), crowded with stands of grass half the height of a horse, punctuated by groves of cottonwood and willow, and attended by half-abandoned river meanders filled with bulrushes and reeds.

Desert-adapted fish glided through its muddy waters, surviving the rushing floods of spring and enduring the sluggish torpor of summer. Fish like the Gila sucker, the humpback chub, and the *Colorado squawfish* ranged through the interconnected desert river systems, living out complicated life cycles that stretched from the burbling chill of the rivers' headwaters to the endless marshes in the delta of the Colorado. Beaver, otters, and a host of other animals made their living along the Gila.

The first European explorers reported a thriving succession of groups living all along the Gila. Most were Pueblo cultures, which greeted the early Spanish explorers amiably enough. Outriders for Francisco Vásquez de Coronado explored the Gila, searching for the fabled and completely fictitious Seven Cities of Gold. Coronado's most valuable and level-headed lieutenant, Melchior Díaz, led a small scouting party hundreds of miles through unknown territory, only to die on the banks of the Gila when impaled on his own lance chasing Indians who had stolen livestock. Franciscans like Father Francisco Garcés and Father Francisco Eusabio Kino traveled repeatedly along the Gila, for the most part winning the admiration of the Indians.

Many of the great names of Western history connect at some point with the Gila River. Early trappers quickly converted the Gila's beavers into hats, which worked a major change on the ecosystem all along the river. Explorers like Jedediah Smith, Kit Carson, Pauline Weaver, and John Walker passed repeatedly along its banks; the famous Mormon Battalion hacked out a wagon road; and General George Kerney's ill-fated Army of the West lugged cannon along its inhospitable banks in an effort to conquer California during the Mexican-American War. Assorted detachments of cavalry chased the elusive Apaches up and down its broad valley, 49ers rushed along its length toward the gold fields of California, and the Butterfield Stage plied its banks until shut down by the Civil War.

A FRAGILE DESERT AT THE MERCY OF HUMAN BEINGS

The long, complex history of the Sonoran Desert demonstrates the intimate connection between geology, ecology, and human beings. Early human cultures depended utterly on the land and learned to survive by making the most of its whims and resources. For a time, it seemed that the Salado, Hohokam, and other desert civilizations had overcome the limitations of their desert home, with great irrigation works, complex civilizations, and far-flung trade networks. But even those civilizations floundered, as a result of a

A MASSACRE THAT SHOCKED THE NATION

One of the most heartrending stories attached to the Gila involves the massacre of the family of Royce Oatman, who set out from Independence, Missouri, in 1850 with his wife and seven children. A successful farmer driven by some fatal restlessness, Royce set out with his family for California, where the gold rush had triggered yearnings all across the continent. They arrived in Tucson in February 1851, already so exhausted that most of their party decided to winter there. But the Oatmans pushed on alone. They made their way down the Santa Cruz River to the villages of the friendly Pima and Maricopa Indians near Gila bend, still 200 grueling miles from the relative safety of the military garrison at Yuma.

After a prospecting adventurer named Dr. John Lecount told them he had just come from Yuma along the Gila and seen no Apaches, Royce resolved to continue. But he underestimated the difficulty of the route, which reduced their progress to a few miles a day. Their oxen grew so exhausted that the Oatmans often had to carry the contents of the wagon uphill by hand. Dr. Lecount found them in this depleted condition about 100 miles from Yuma. He promised to hurry on to Yuma and send back help. Thus encouraged, they floundered on.

Several days after leaving the Oatmans, Lecount encountered a group of Apache warriors. He kept his weapons at hand, but they stole his horse during the night. He left a note for Royce on a tree and hurried on to Yuma for help.

The Oatmans encountered the same Indians, shortly after making yet another crossing of the capricious, meandering river. The Indians demanded food, which Oatman reluctantly provided. He then urged his family to show courage and go about their business with nonchalance. It proved the wrong tactic. After a brief conference, the Indians fell suddenly on the small family, killing most of them immediately. They spared only the two teenaged daughters, Olive and Mary Ann. They also inadvertently spared their brother, Lorenzo, who was knocked unconscious by a savage blow to the head and left for dead. Fortunately, two Pima Indians found him and rescued him.

The Apaches sold the girls to a band of Mohave Indians for two horses and a blanket. The girls lived as semi-slaves among the Mohaves on the Colorado River for six years, during which time Mary Ann starved to death. Meanwhile, their brother continued to chase rumors of white girls held captive among the Mohave and to offer a reward for their return. Eventually, this prompted a Yuma man to enlist a Mohave Indian's aid. The Indian bought Olive from the Mohaves and reunited her with Lorenzo. The tragedy made national headlines and became the subject for a lurid, best-selling book, *The Captivity of the Oatman Girls*, still widely available in Arizona bookstores.

combination of conflict, overpopulation, and the climatic cycles that have always shadowed the Sonoran Desert.

Now, the Sonoran Desert is the most populated desert in the world, with major cities like Phoenix and Tucson set in its heart. Those cities rely on a combination of ice age groundwater pumped out of wells hundreds of feet deep and water trapped in reservoirs and transported across hundreds of miles of desert in great canals. The dams and irrigation canals have destroyed or degraded an estimated 90 percent of desert riparian areas like the Gila River. Moreover, activities like cattle grazing have converted huge swaths of grassland into desert.

Meanwhile, the pollution-spurred warming of the planet could significantly increase the duration and severity of droughts, which tree-ring studies demonstrate could last 30 years or more even before the most recent rise in global temperatures. The rapidly growing cities of the Sonoran Desert are likely to face hard choices and grave challenges in the decades to come. Let's hope they have better luck than the Hohokam.

Mojave Desert

California, Arizona

The Mojave Desert is a jagged, angular land of staggering extremes. It contains the lowest, hottest place in North America, a great underground river, places of bizarre beauty, a terrible earthquake fault, dead lakes, low basins, and strange and resourceful plants and animals. It occupies some 51,000 square miles (81,000 square km) and extends from the east slopes of the Sierra Nevada to the Colorado plateau before merging with the Great Basin Desert to the north and the Sonoran Desert to the south and southeast.

The two most common causes of desert combine in the Mojave to create an especially harsh and austere environment.

First, it lies along the line of latitude that spawns deserts all around the globe, due to the atmospheric circulation patterns that cause warm moist air to rise at the equator, drop its moisture in tropical rains, flow toward the poles until it cools, and downdrafts to the surface, largely stripped of moisture. Such a pattern causes deserts all around the world in both the Northern Hemisphere and the Southern Hemisphere.

Second, the Mojave lies behind walls of mountains, which force moisture-laden air from the ocean to rise, cool, condense, and lose moisture before sweeping back down the landward side of those mountain chains, further drying out the already sun-blasted landscape of the Mojave. To the east of the Mojave, the Sierra Nevadas rise to create a chain of peaks towering to some 14,000 feet (4,667 m). The Sierra Nevadas were created when the collision of two massive crustal plates caused a series of massive islands to smash into the edge of the North American crustal plate, causing the gigantic landmasses to buckle and fold. Prior to that geologic event, the western edge of North America consisted of a series of low, flat coastal plains. The ocean periodically swallowed up these great plains during warm periods when sea levels rose. This turned the low plains into a land of shallow seas, gigantic lakes, and rolling grasslands during glacial periods, when the growth of the polar ice caps locked up so much water that sea levels dropped worldwide.

The Joshua tree, a relative of the yucca, largely defines the cold, harsh Mojave Desert of North America. The bristling, waxy spines of the Joshua tree can survive both prolonged drought and extended winter freezes. *(Peter Aleshire)*

A COLLISION OF CONTINENTS

This collision of continents created the topography of the western United States and Mexico. Initially, the collision built up the Sierra Nevadas, pasted California and parts of Washington and Oregon onto the western edge of North America, and isolated the terrain that would one day become the deserts of North America behind this rain-stealing rampart of rising granite. Later, the forces driving this collision from deep beneath the surface shifted, causing the Pacific plate to start sliding north toward the North American plate. The resulting shearing force fractured the surface of Earth, creating the San Andreas Fault, which runs from the Gulf of California up to San Francisco. Now the two plates moved past one another at about the speed fingernails grow. This titanic, ongoing movement created the modern landscape of the American Southwest. These forces stretched and pulled the surface, which created a whole series of north-south mountain ranges, separated by low basins. This *basin and*

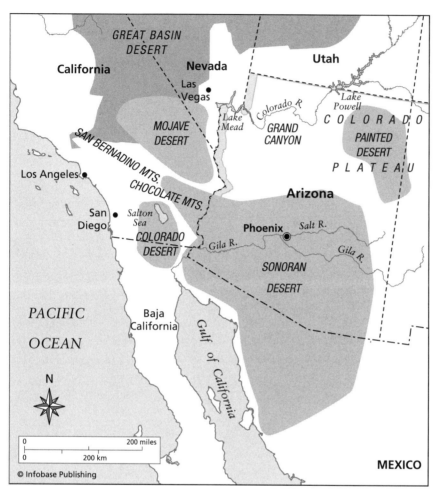

Deserts of the western United States

range topography runs throughout the four deserts of North America, including the Mojave.

After this continental stretching and sinking created the basic pattern of the southwestern landscape, periods of uplift took place. By the time they had finished, the shifts had created the differences in elevation that distinguish the four great American deserts. (An example can be seen in the color insert on page C-1).

About 20 million years ago, due to changing plate motions out west, a great slab of what would one day become the western United States began a rapid rise. The uplifting continues to this day in a huge area centered on the Four Corners region where Utah, Arizona, Colorado, and New Mexico meet. The rising Colorado Plateau is a sprawling region just west and south of the Rocky Mountains. As it rose, the Colorado

River cut the Grand Canyon from its leading edge as it ran its long course down toward the Gulf of California. Along its course farther south, it largely defines the boundary between the Mojave and the Sonoran deserts.

Some 2 million years ago, another period of uplift separated the Mojave Desert from the much larger and lusher Sonoran Desert. This shift made the Mojave Desert transitional between the lower, largely snow-free, summer monsoon–graced Sonoran Desert and the high, cold, desolate Great Basin Desert.

This sequence of geologic events created a landscape of dramatic extremes in the Mojave Desert. The Mojave's dry, hot summers and sometimes frost-prone winters exclude many of the desert-adapted species of the Sonoran Desert, like the distinctive saguaro cactus. Instead, the world's largest yucca, the Joshua tree, serves as the signature plant of the Mojave Desert.

Two national monuments capture those extremes: Death Valley and Joshua Tree National Monument.

THE WORLD IN A SONG

The Mojave Desert–dwelling Chemuehevi Indians had few possessions, but they always had their songs. The Chemuehevi lived in the deep desert, hunting rats, rabbits, and bighorn sheep, gathering roots, tubers, beans, and berries and moving ceaselessly over a broad area. They thrived for thousands of years in desert that routinely killed settlers trying to cross it. They relied on a deep knowledge of the landscape and its resources and a few simple possessions. The most treasured inheritance of any Chemuehevi was the inherited song of his clan. These songs were really elaborate stories that often took years to memorize and days to sing. The stories accounted for the origins of the smallest features of the landscape in a vivid, funny, intricate mythology.

The songs also contained a deep code, an oral map of the desert landscape that pinpointed the location of every stream, water-filled wash, hollowed rock, prickly pear patch, or other seasonal resources. A person who knew the song that went with a certain area always knew how to find water and vital resources.

Other groups wishing to pass through the domain of the Chemuehevi would seek out the clan that claimed the territory and effectively pay a member of that claim to accompany the group through the territory. This was simple self-interest, since few people could last long in the desert without the map to the vital resources and water sources contained in the clan's song.

DEATH VALLEY: THE LOWEST, HOTTEST PLACE

The spectacularly eroded Death Valley is a strange desert in a continental sinkhole that remains one of the most bizarre and forbidding places in the world. Pine-clad mountains harboring the oldest trees on Earth overlook the breathtaking plunge into a valley that ranks as the lowest, hottest, and driest place in North America.

The rocks in and around Death Valley have a much longer history than the valley itself, which is relatively young. Some of the rocks in the surrounding mountains are more than 500 million years old, formed miles beneath the Earth before the first living things crawled out onto dry land. Those deeply buried rocks were thrust upward through miles of rock into their present positions. These *Precambrian* rocks include *gneiss*, schist, granite, and some volcanic rocks dating back 1.8 billion years.

In *Mesozoic* times (245 million to 65 million years ago), the quiet, sea-covered continental margin was replaced by erupting volcanoes, up-lifting mountains, and compressional thrust faulting. These changes were brought about by a tectonic collision to the west when the western edge of the North American continent was pushed against the oceanic plate under the Pacific Ocean. As the dinosaurs died out, the mammals flour-ished, the Ice Ages came and went, and Death Valley and the whole of the Mojave Desert region changed dramatically. During the 1.8-million-year-long progression of Ice Ages, Death Valley filled with lakes, along with camels, deer, rhinoceroses, titanotheres, and three-toed horses. But the rise of the Sierra Nevadas some 25 million years ago began to trans-form the valley into a desert. The surge of the Earth provoked numerous volcanic eruptions, sometimes blanketing the entire region in ash and cre-ating a complex network of new faults and fractures.

Death Valley is bounded by long, deep, active earthquake faults. Such faults mark the place where the Earth has been stretched, strained, and cracked. Pressures from beneath cause the crust to crack along such faults, which often allows mountain ranges to rise. When a chunk of the Earth between two such mountain-range-raising faults splits lose and drops down as the land on either side rises, it is called a *graben*. That makes Death Valley one of the most dramatic grabens on the planet. So although the mountains overlooking the valley rise to 11,000 feet (3,667 m), the floor of Death Valley is actually 282 feet (94 m) below sea level. The valley itself didn't begin to open up along these fault lines until some 4 million years ago, when the faults lifted the mountains and dropped the valley floor. The shift caused dramatic changes all around the valley. For instance, the lake bottom deposits laid down in earlier wet periods were lifted high above the valley floor as the mountains rose and the floor sank, to intrigue future generations of geologists.

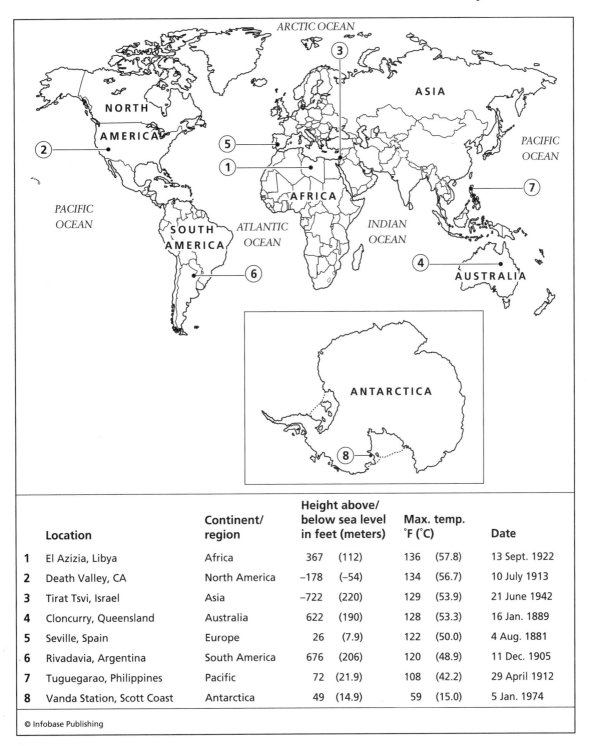

	Location	Continent/ region	Height above/ below sea level in feet (meters)		Max. temp. °F (°C)		Date
1	El Azizia, Libya	Africa	367	(112)	136	(57.8)	13 Sept. 1922
2	Death Valley, CA	North America	−178	(−54)	134	(56.7)	10 July 1913
3	Tirat Tsvi, Israel	Asia	−722	(220)	129	(53.9)	21 June 1942
4	Cloncurry, Queensland	Australia	622	(190)	128	(53.3)	16 Jan. 1889
5	Seville, Spain	Europe	26	(7.9)	122	(50.0)	4 Aug. 1881
6	Rivadavia, Argentina	South America	676	(206)	120	(48.9)	11 Dec. 1905
7	Tuguegarao, Philippines	Pacific	72	(21.9)	108	(42.2)	29 April 1912
8	Vanda Station, Scott Coast	Antarctica	49	(14.9)	59	(15.0)	5 Jan. 1974

© Infobase Publishing

World's hottest places by continent/region

Although the mountains tower above the sunken valley, they are really only the shattered remnants of mountains that have eroded away. In fact, the floor of Death Valley is still sinking and the mountains are still rising due to the continued strain and stretch of Earth's crust. The erosion of the surrounding mountains has filled the still-sinking Death Valley with some 10,000 feet (3,300 m) of sediment. Taking that 10,000 feet shaved off the top of the mountains and deposited into the valley into account, the mountains around Death Valley have been pushed upward a total of nearly four miles.

All of the debris carried off the mountains by running water has ended up in Death Valley, which is so low that no streams can run out of it. Such low-lying valleys with "interior drainage" are a hallmark of deserts. In wet cycles such as Ice Ages, they often hold huge, freshwater lakes. In dry cycles when the planet warms, they become scorching deserts.

In fact, one key definition of a desert is a region where the evaporation exceeds the annual rainfall. For instance, trapped in the rain shadow of the Sierra Nevadas, Death Valley receives only about 1.7 inches (43 mm) of rain per year. However, it is so low and hot that a lake in the bottom of Death Valley would lose 12.5 feet (4.1 m) of water per year to evaporation. So even the streams that run down off the imposing surrounding mountains quickly vanish into the thirsty sands of Death Valley.

This strange geologic history has made Death Valley the most extreme place in the Mojave Desert, with its mere trace of rain, blazing hot summers, and frigid winters. It has also created a bizarre collection of geological wonders, which includes Badwater, at 282 feet (94 m) below sea level, the lowest place in North America. The deepest, youngest place in the valley, Badwater began gaping open and sinking some 3 million years ago. Nonetheless, the gravel and sand washed out of the surrounding mountains have accumulated in a layer 8,000 feet (2,667 m) deep.

This nearly two-mile-deep (3.2 km) layer of rocks and debris is covered by a thick layer of silt and salt. The water that washes out of the surrounding mountains and comes finally to this lowest place contains dissolved salt and minerals. But the water evaporates quickly from the soil, leaving behind those salts and minerals. The result is the great Death Valley Salt Pan, an amazingly flat expanse that in the winter collects a shallow sheen of water far saltier than the ocean and in the summer hardens to a salt flat.

Northwest of this low point lies Devils' Golf Course, a bed of solid rock salt that is the remains of Lake Manly, which was 90 miles (144 km) long and 600 feet (200 m) deep before drying up as the last Ice Age ended some 8,000 years ago, leaving behind its salt and minerals. The bed of the vanished lake is now covered with a 3–6-foot-thick (1–2 m) layer of salt. Portions of the salt bed that are above the water table and out of reach of the infrequent floods have dissolved into a strange landscape of pinnacles and spires.

Death Valley also contains valuable deposits of a chemical salt called *borax*, once vital in making ceramic glazes, fertilizer, glass, fiberglass, solder, water softeners, and some drugs. The borax leaches out of volcanic ash in superheated volcanic hot springs. Such hot springs fumed and steamed beneath Death Valley for millions of years as a result of all the geological upheaval, which left layers of borax up to 200 feet (67 m) thick. Fractures and uplift cracked open the layers of borax, and rain dissolved the mineral salts, carried them to the valley floor, and then deposited thick layers as the water evaporated. This layer of mineral salt spurred one of the few viable industries in Death Valley, a borax mining operation that scraped off the surface of the salt pan, purified it, dried it, and shipped it to the waiting world in great wagons hauled by 20-mule teams.

Another oddity on the floor of Death Valley is the Racetrack Playa, which features seemingly impossible wind-pushed rocks that have slid great distances on a perfectly flat plain. Strangely enough, no one has actually seen the rocks move, but their tracks are perfectly preserved in the hardened mud of the flat surface. Geologists have not settled on one explanation for the mystery, but one theory suggests that the occasional combination of ice, a slippery flat surface, and wind are responsible for the movement. The rocks sit on an extremely smooth, nearly flat surface of fine-grained silt. About once in every 10 years, a severe winter storm will cover the Racetrack Playa with about a foot of water. Usually, such winter storms bring a cold front in their wake, resulting in a sharp drop in temperature. In that case, ice can form around the edges of the rock and on the surface of the water collected in the playa. As the desert warms up and this layer of ice thaws, some of the rocks will end up on their own little ice raft. A strong wind can push this ice raft, often with the rock dragging a projecting knob, which cuts a path through the silt of the surface. The result is a rock sitting in the middle of a seemingly perfectly level mud-crack playa, with the track of its passage over the silt plainly visible along its path.

DESERT-ADAPTED SPECIES STRUGGLE

Death Valley also boasts an array of desert-adapted Mojave species, despite its harsh conditions, even in seemingly impossible places like Badwater. Periodically, storms create shallow, fleeting ponds on the salt flat, full of minerals and salt. But that is just fine with soldier flies, which lay their eggs in the salt flats so their larvae will hatch and wiggle across the bottom in a biological sprint against the drying of the fleeting pond. Algae blooms and fat bronze water beetles plunge into the fleeting pools to graze, breathing through antenna projecting out into the air. Brine flies

Desert bighorn sheep work their way along a volcanic ridge alongside the Colorado River. They are so perfectly adapted to the desert that they can go a week without a drink even in the 120 degree F summer and then regain 40 percent of their body weight in one long drink. They were nearly exterminated by hunters and diseases carried by domestic sheep, but in the past century have been reintroduced to desert mountain ranges throughout Arizona. *(Peter Aleshire)*

also seemingly miraculously appear in the ephemeral pools, thriving on levels of salts and minerals that would quickly kill most other creatures. Such brine flies live in these alkaline pools throughout the West, forming the base of a quick-acting food chain. The larvae attach themselves to the bottom and grow a long tube out of their back end that reaches to the surface as a breathing tube. They eventually pupate into their adult fly form and escape to the surface in a bubble of air. They then fly off, seeking nectar and pollen.

CREOSOTE: THE OLDEST ON EARTH

One of the most widespread plants in the Mojave and Sonoran Deserts is the creosote bush, which nourishes its own interdependent set of creatures. Remarkably, the creosote might live longer than any other plant on the planet, nearly 12,000 years. That is remarkable considering the low, olive-green bush with tiny leaves thrives in areas too tough for almost any other plant. A biologist working in the Mojave Desert noticed what seemed to be a great ring of creosote bushes. Intrigued, he took samples of plants all around the circle and also dug up some fragments of wood from a mound in the center of the circle. He discovered that all of the bushes in the circle were genetically identical. Then he discovered that the wood in the center of the circle was nearly 12,000 years old. From this, he concluded that the creosote bushes growing around the ring were offshoots from the roots of that original plant, which means the original plant was still alive and still flourishing as many connected bushes after 12,000 years. There is something encouraging about the idea that a plant clinging to survival in such a hard place and growing only an inch a year could through sheer persistence hang on to become the world's oldest living thing.

Remarkable adaptations enable the creosote to survive in places where it does not rain for a year at a time and summer temperatures soar to 130°F (54°C). The creosote can send roots down 150 feet (50 m) to find groundwater. Normally, the moisture difference between roots in groundwater and the sun-blasted leaves of a plant create a pressure difference between root and leaves called osmotic pressure. The creosote can stand a greater pressure difference between leaf and root than any other living plant, which means it can draw water from deeper in the soil without rupturing the cells that feed the water to the leaves. The leaves also have many chemicals that protect them from the sun, *dehydration*, and insects. These chemicals can also serve as a natural herbicide, to keep other plants from growing too close and competing for the scarce water. Native Americans learned to use some of these substances for medicines, sealants, glue, and other purposes. They also made adroit use of the insects that made use of the creosote; for instance, they used a protective chemical secreted by a flat, scale insect that lives only on creosote to mend pottery, waterproof baskets, and glue arrowheads.

Many other desert dwellers have also developed ways to deal with those defensive plant chemicals and make full use of the creosote. The creosote bagworm moth lays her eggs in the small leaves of the creosote then stitches the leaf together with silk. The larvae eventually hatch and promptly make a meal of their leafy home. The archenemy of the creosote bagworm is the bracconid wasp, which looks for these sewn-together creosote leaves and then lays her own eggs on top of the moth larva. The hatching wasp larvae consume the bagworm moth larvae before they get a chance to dine on creosote leaf, which provides a glimpse of the ecological complexity of such crucial plants in so hard a place as a desert.

ICE AGE DESERT FISH HANGS ON

Death Valley also harbors one of the more inconspicuous but fascinating of endangered species, the Devils Hole Pupfish. These minnowlike, almost transparent, 1.5-inch-long (38.1 mm) fish with odd, bright blue eyes live in a single, spring-fed pool that has collected in a collapsed limestone cavern. They are descended from cyprinodonts, fish that once lived in the many Ice Age lakes and streams connected by runoff and tributaries throughout the Southwest. As the climate shifted, the glaciers melted, and grasslands gave way to desert, lakes evaporated and streams withered. Scattered populations of fish held on in isolated, spring-fed pools like Devils Hole. They had spent millions of years living in these lakes and streams, but in a mere 8,000 years they adapted to much warmer water temperatures and salinities six times greater than in the ocean. In the process, the surviving populations separated into a dozen different species, all of which are now critically endangered.

The remarkable adaptation of the pupfish has provided biologists with an intriguing example of how rapidly mutations can prompt evolutionary change when a species is faced with an ecological crisis. Moreover, the pupfish and their kin also adapted to cope with high mineral levels in the water, like calcium. As a result, biologists hope that studying the pupfish may help them develop ways to prevent the overload of calcium salts that causes kidney stones and kidney failure in humans. The Devils Hole pupfish are especially important in solving these physiological and evolutionary mysteries because they became isolated in their small pool even before the ice ages faded. Most of their relatives, like the pupfish in the Amargosa Valley, Salt Creek, and the Owens River, were separated much later and so are genetically almost identical.

JOSHUA TREE NATIONAL MONUMENT: AS LUSH AS THE MOJAVE GETS

While Death Valley represents the most extreme environment in the Mojave Desert, Joshua Tree National Monument in Southern California presents the Mojave at its balmy best. Of course, this is relative, since this high-elevation desert with its giants' playground of granite boulders and an octopus's garden of bizarre yucca swelters in summer, freezes in winter, and qualifies in every way as a desert.

Still, it seems a biologically rich wonderland, thanks largely to the exuberant presence of that trademark plant of the Mojave Desert, the Joshua tree, which seems like a mutant yucca on steroids. Joshua trees remain the most distinctive visual clue to the Mojave. Few grow in the Sonoran Desert, where the saguaro remains the distinctive plant. And few grow in the Great Basin Desert, which is too cold and dry. So the presence of the Joshua trees marks the Mojave as a transitional desert between the low, warm Sonoran and the high, cold Great Basin.

Early travelers called them dagger trees, because of the furious cluster of sharp-tipped spines serving as leaves. But Mormon settlers who in the 1800s spread throughout much of the Southwest looking for their own promised land where they could escape religious persecution called them Joshua trees after their great prophet.

The desert-dwelling Kawaiisu Indians account for the Joshua tree with a story. They say that Coyote and his brother were being chased by enemies, when they made their escape by turning their many angry foes into Joshua trees. When Coyote and his brother reached the end of the world, they in turn were turned into two stones. These stones sometimes bang together, causing the earthquakes that plague this area. Interestingly enough, the nearby San Andreas Fault runs within 100 miles (161 km) of this high desert and heads toward the ocean, just as the myth suggests.

Joshua trees are considered *monocotyledons*, which means that they don't branch in regular patterns like roses or ivy. Instead, Joshua trees put out arms haphazardly, which makes each plant distinct. They usually grow on a straight fibrous trunk for about 10 feet (3 m) before putting out their first branch, after which they branch in weird and creative profusion. A trip through a Joshua tree forest seems like a fantasy world journey, with each tangled, twisted, bristling tree harboring some individual, strange tale.

In the spring, the branches sport creamy white flowers. Each flower opens for only a single night, hoping to lure a species of yucca moth that specializes in fertilizing Joshua trees in a striking example of one of the most intricate and puzzling relationships in nature. The female yucca moth visits a sequence of yucca flowers, gathering up pollen and rolling it into a ball under her head. At the next flower, she lays an egg at the base and then crawls up the flower and deliberately brushes the tip or stigma of the flower with her head, fertilizing the blossom with the pollen she brought from other flowers. The pollinated Joshua tree then produces seed pods, which contain the moth's eggs. Her larva eventually hatch, safe in the seed pod. When they hatch, they find the table already set with a banquet of Joshua tree seeds. They feast on the seeds in the pod, but somehow always leave some seeds behind.

The specialized relationship between the yucca and the yucca moth is one of the most remarkable examples of a symbiotic relationship, in which each partner helps the other. The mother moth that gathers the pollen does not eat either the pollen or the nectar. Many insects visit flowers to eat the nectar and in the process get dusted with the pollen. When they visit the next flower, they inadvertently fertilize the next plant while grubbing about for the nectar. But the adult yucca moths get no direct benefit from visiting the flowers and gathering up a ball of pollen and nectar. Instead, this whole complex sequence of actions directly benefits the Joshua tree, which then benefits her offspring. Pollinating the Joshua tree stimulates the development of the seed pods that feed the moth's larvae. Just to finish the strangely deliberate element of this mutually beneficial relationship, the larvae do not eat all the seeds, which enables the Joshua tree to reproduce. Of course, biologists believe that the yucca moth has developed this elaborate behavior through a long process of natural selection, so that the behavior is hardwired into the moth's DNA rather than the result of conscious thought. But the interaction is so intimate that each species of yucca now has its own species of yucca moth. Neither the yucca nor the moth could survive without the other.

These remarkable plants dominate the landscape of Joshua Tree National Monument, one of the most biologically diverse areas in the entire Mojave Desert.

THE EDGE OF THE DESERT

The monument lies on the southwestern border of the Mojave Desert. To the south lies the Colorado Desert, a division of the Sonoran Desert that includes Palm Springs, the Coachella Valley, and the Salton Sea, which in the Ice Age rivaled Lake Manly and which is now sustained mostly with irrigation water brought in from the Colorado River and used to grow most of the nation's winter vegetables. That once-mighty Ice Age lake returned from the dead between 1904 and 1907 when a break in an irrigation dike on the Colorado River caused the whole flow of the Colorado River to take a hard right-hand turn into the low-lying Coachella Valley. Desperate engineers finally sealed the breach and returned the river to its former path by building an elevated railway track across the breach and then dumping freight cars loaded with rock into the gap.

The Joshua tree area stands at an elevation of about 2,500 feet (833 m) above sea level, while the nearby Salton Sea is 235 feet (78 m) below sea level. The uplift in the 50–100 mile (80–160 km) span between these two landmarks defines the boundary between the Mojave and the Sonoran. It is a result of the tug, pull, stretch, and uplift along that tempestuous boundary between the Pacific and the North American crustal plates. The San Andreas Fault runs along the edge of that uplift dividing Mojave from Sonoran. Down in Palm Springs, the 11,000-foot-tall (3,667 m) San Jacinto Mountains on the south side of the valley were formed from a great bubble of granite several hundred miles to the south in what is now Mexico. As the mountain range rose, it moved north along the fault. On the north side of the Palm Springs area lie the much older San Gorgonio Mountains.

The continent continues to split apart along this fault line dividing the Sonoran from the Mojave. The San Andreas Fault, which starts in the sea bottom beneath the Gulf of California, is now a transverse fault, which means its two sides are moving past one another. But shifts in the mantle could easily change it back into a more conventional rift system, so that the long narrow Gulf of California could one day gape open to become a new Atlantic Ocean, splitting off much of California to become another wandering continent like Australia.

So the forces that define the edge of the North American crustal plate have also caused the Mojave Desert and Joshua Tree National Monument to rise in the past 15 to 11 million years. The mountains in this desert are formed of strikingly different rocks from Death Valley. They are mostly made of Mesozoic granite, molten rock forged, cooled, and crystallized miles beneath the surface between 240 and 65 million years ago. These rocks contain gleaming crystals of feldspar and a crisscrossing of fine white veins, made by molten quartz that squeezed into cracks in the deeply buried rock to eventually cool and harden into these bright veins. This deeply buried mass of molten rock was forced to the surface by deeper forces, perhaps going down 100 miles (160 km) to currents in the semi-molten mantle. The mass of rock rose either in great blocks or in dikes and ridges along fractures in the cooler, overlying rock.

Once the uplift that formed the basin and range province and the Colorado Plateau set in, these now-hard, igneous intrusions were lifted high above sea level. Now much harder than the surrounding sedimentary rock, erosion went to work like a sculptor. Erosion exposed these masses of crystallized rock to sunlight and littered the landscape with gargantuan piles of boulders.

The landscape in Joshua Tree National Monument consists of sculptural boulder piles interspersed with the equally otherworldly Joshua trees. These massive buried slabs of granite were often cracked and fractured in regular ways by the forces that uplifted them. Geologists believe that most of these low-angle extension faults formed some 30 million years ago when these rocks were still buried and the shifts at the edge of the continent were stretching the basin and range province to the breaking point. Erosion along these often regular, parallel fractures at the surface caused the boulder piles to weather into dramatic shapes and piles. Although they are called boulder piles, in fact these dramatic outcrops are generally formed of a single mass of cracked rock, so that the boulders remain connected to one another in the pile. Moreover, they are rounded by the flaking away of the large crystals in the granite matrix, rather than having been rolled in a river or succession of floods, which is what produces most rounded boulder shapes.

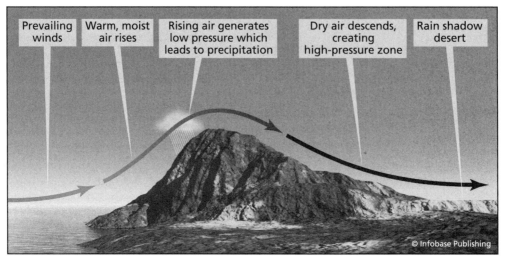

Rain shadow desert

These striking boulder piles have formed in a gap between two mountain ranges, each uplifted by a sharp fault line. Like Death Valley, the desert area in the Monument is a graben, a block of land between two faults that has dropped as the mountains on either side rose. To the south, the Little San Bernardino Mountains are made of 1.8-billion-year-old gneiss, ancient seafloor deposits that were deeply buried, melted down, cooled, and thrust once again to the surface. Somewhere in that process the buried gneiss was invaded by molten granite, which is identical in composition to most types of lava and ash, but which never reached the surface before hardening.

All the rocks that were laid down between 500 million and 25 million years ago in the area have vanished. This means that the region was uplifted and all of these older rocks were eroded and carried off. However, the area did not become a desert until relatively recent times. It was probably a shrub-filled grassland until continued geological upheaval raised a low range of mountains that cut off the flow of moist air from the ocean, creating the conditions for a rain shadow desert. Although the area probably returned to grassland during the wet glacial periods, the dwindling of the Ice Ages some 10,000 years ago converted it into a high, cold, biologically distinctive desert.

DESERT BURSTS INTO FLOWER

The Joshua tree represents one set of adaptations to a place with dry summers and chilling, but still thirsty, winters. Desert creatures have developed many different solutions to those problems. For instance, desert wildflowers seem almost miraculous in their delicate abundance during a rare wet year, when a succession of winter rains or snows yields to the crescendo of spring rain. Suddenly, the seemingly lifeless sand and gravel of the desert soil erupts with a riotous bloom of frail red, blue, purple, and orange flowers.

In fact, this desert soil harbors somewhere between 100 and 2,400 seeds in every square foot. Although harvester ants and their seed-loving neighbors like kangaroo rats consume perhaps 95 percent of these seeds, enough remain dormant and waiting to cause a riot of color in the monochrome desert every five to 10 years when the conditions are just right. Each of the seeds can hold its store of moisture and potential growth through years of barren springs until just the right succession of soaking rains dissolves a coating on the outside that inhibits *germination*. Each seed has its own carefully programmed instructions in the form of DNA, which include requirements for everything from winter rain to the salt content of the soil. This reluctance to sprout until the conditions are perfect ensures that the seed can give rise to a healthy plant that can last long enough in the face of the short, bittersweet desert spring to release a fresh generation of patient seeds. Some produce seeds exquisitely designed to win that lethal race against the blight of summer. For instance, the seed of the corksbill has a corkscrew tail that coils and uncoils with a change in humidity. The resulting motion effectively screws the seed down into the ground, where it is more likely to avoid the attentions of ants and kangaroo rats.

Oddly enough, the flowers that seem so out of place in a desert help sustain the desert. Certainly, anyone who has witnessed spring in the desert has marveled at the sudden bounty in these normally dry and lifeless soils. How can anything so luminous and delicate as a desert poppy find enough moisture to survive here? So researchers recently did a large-scale study of how much water desert flowers use in such a bountiful spring bloom. They found that the flowers essentially use every bit of excess water that falls in an unusually wet year, so that almost none of this glut of rain makes it past the root zone of the annual plants to reach the water table. In fact, the bloom of the annuals in a good year may actually use up all the moisture that falls, which means that the flowers themselves dry out the soil and help ensure that the area remains a desert by gulping down most of the excess rainfall.

IT TAKES A FUNGUS TO MAKE A SOIL

Fortunately for the thirsty flowers, they get help from strange fungi waiting in the top two inches of these desert soils. In wet, fertile areas, the topsoil is constantly enriched by the carbon-containing debris of plants, including leaves, roots, and twigs. In the riotously productive rain forest, the mass of plant debris on the ground supports such a population

RATTLESNAKES: DEADLY ADAPTATIONS

The diamondback rattlesnake is one of the most feared desert reptiles, but bee stings kill far more Americans each year than rattlesnake bites. In fact, rattlesnakes almost always give fair warning before striking and remain essential to the desert ecosystem, since they keep the rodent population in check that would otherwise decimate struggling plants. *(Peter Aleshire)*

Although rattlesnakes evolved long before the world's deserts took their present form, they were exquisitely preadapted to desert conditions. The fear of rattlesnakes is greatly exaggerated, since far more people die from bee stings or dog bites than rattlesnake venom. But something about the coiled warning, slitted eyes, and flicking tongue of the venomous rattlesnake, a type of pit viper, stirs a deep-seated fear in many people.

In truth, rattlesnakes are a marvel of evolution. The toxic saliva they interject through their hollow, needle-sharp, wickedly curved, and pointed fangs contains a mixture of enzymes unique to pit vipers. These enzymes paralyze muscles, destroy blood vessels, and actually start the digestive process before the snake even swallows its prey. They are one of the few creatures with dual visual systems, since they can spot prey with either their eyes or with infrared detecting, heat-sensitive pits in their upper jaws, giving them the real-world equivalent of the color-coded vision of the monster in the movie *Predator*. They can detect the heat of a candle from 30 feet away and detect rodents like kangaroo rats that remain their favorite meal even in the pitch-dark desert night when they do most of their hunting. These heat-detecting pits can sense temperature differences of a fraction of a degree at the range of the snake's coiled strike. Rattlesnakes strike, let their venom work, then slither up, unhinge their jaws, and swallow their prey whole. They cannot eat larger creatures, so when they strike a human being it is only after attempts to warn off the threat with their trademark rattles have failed. The rattles, which can vibrate up to 60 times a second, are composed of the same fibrous protein as a human's fingernails, and the snake gets another rattle every time it sheds another layer of skin. Half the time, when they bite a creature as large as a human being they do not even bother to interject venom. Recent research has suggested that mother rattlesnakes may hang about their nests for a week or more to protect their newborns.

Most people bitten by rattlesnakes survive, even without treatment. Moreover, most people who get bitten provoke the bite. One Phoenix emergency room physician recalled one case involving a rattlesnake bite. A young man with a pet rattlesnake got drunk and started showing off to his friends. He bent down close to his pet rattlesnake and flicked his tongue out at the snake. So the snake bit him on the tongue. Still drunk and befuddled, the young man had heard an old wives' tale that suggested an electrical current can break down rattlesnake venom. So he went out to the garage and had a friend wire his swollen tongue to the battery of his truck. Naturally enough, that only made things much worse. The drunk and foolish man ended up in the hospital, where antivenom saved his life.

of bacteria, insects, fungus, and other plants that few of these nutrients remain in the soil. In most other areas, the nutrients provided by decay of plant matter build up in the topsoil. Unfortunately, desert soils get very few nutrients from decaying plants. Termites gobble the bits and pieces of wood, harvester ants and rodents gather up every scrap of plant remains, and the dry, harsh climate limits the ability of soil bacteria to break down the remaining organic debris.

Desert soils do have unique species of fungi. Most desert soils are graced by a fungus that grows in the top few inches of soil that engulf the sand grains. These *fungal hyphae* form a vital, symbiotic relationship with the usually short, struggling roots of desert plants. The fungus colonizes the roots of the plant, and the plant and the fungus then cooperate to grow little tendrils called mycorrhizae that envelop the root. This fungal add-on increases the root's ability to absorb moisture tenfold, maximizing the yield for the plant in the dry desert soil. In return, the plant creates energy from sunlight in its leaves and feeds the buried fungus. As a sort of final tip, the fungus also helps the roots absorb essential minerals like phosphorus, zinc, and copper, normally scarce in the impoverished desert soils. This interdependent soil chemistry helps account for the extraordinary delicacy of many desert soils. For instance, during World War II, General George Patton's troops practiced tank maneuvers in many areas of the Mojave Desert. Now some 60 years later, the tank tracks remain clearly visible in the slow-healing desert soil because the tanks destroyed the fungal networks and prevented any other plants from taking root.

GRAND CANYON: A TRANSFORMED SLIVER OF THE MOJAVE

The mile-deep gash of the Grand Canyon connects the drought-adapted Mojave Desert to the frost-adapted Great Basin Desert. As shown in the color insert on page C-2, the desert plants and animals in the bottom of the canyon have evolved to adapt to the odd combination of desert heat and rampaging river in the course of the canyon's five-million-year history, especially in the 10,000 years since the last ice age. However, no change has been as rapid or complex in its effects as the construction of a dam that has transformed the nature of the river as it twists and turns through the 277 miles (446 km) of the Grand Canyon.

That is especially true for the strange assemblage of desert fish that adapted to the moods of the warm, flood-prone river from the once-massive delta in the Gulf of California to its cold, clear origins in the Rocky Mountains. Once upon a time, strange fish with whiskers, humps, fleshy lips, and giant tails ruled the capricious, silt-choked, flood-prone Colorado River. They thrived for millennia despite enormous floods,

The Grand Canyon provides a linear expansion of the characteristic Mojave Desert plants deep into both the Sonoran and Great Basin Deserts, providing hot Mojave Desert conditions in its 277-mile-long (446 km), mile-deep canyon. *(Peter Aleshire)*

warm water, and silt so thick they often had little use for eyes. Then came the engineers, the dams, and remorseless invaders like trout, carp, and catfish. The world of the besieged native Colorado River fish changed abruptly, and the six-foot-long (2 m) *squawfish*, the pout-faced flannel-mouth suckers, and the strangely shaped humpback chubs all but disappeared from the desert rivers they once dominated. On the Colorado, they held out mostly in the tributaries where conditions had remained largely unchanged since the waning of the Ice Age.

The Colorado River has been transformed by a series of dams that have eliminated the silt-laden spring floods that once increased the flow of the river 100-fold. Once, the river could carry 27 million tons of mud past a given point in a single day and was commonly described as too thick to drink and too thin to plow. Once, the river temperature varied dramatically from summer to winter. Now, however, water released from the bottom of Lake Powell keeps the river's temperature frigid and constant all year round. Moreover, nonnative fish adapted to the cold temperatures, lack of silt, and lack of floods now dominate the river.

The changes caused by the dam have altered the ecosystem in the Grand Canyon, creating hosts of winners and losers. Trout have thrived, squawfish have disappeared. Salt cedar has exploded, willows have retreated. Beavers have boomed, otters have vanished. On one hand, the clear water and the tamed floods have made the streamside ecosystem more productive by causing a population explosion at the base of the aquatic food chain. On the other hand, the surges of water released each day to generate electricity for faraway cities also threaten to strip sand from beaches, eroding the foundation of the whole system in the long term.

The most dramatic ecological changes took place in the water column, where the temperature plunged and the rush of light fostered sweeping changes. Bottom-growing forests of cladophora, a green alga, spread rapidly throughout the river. This ubiquitous green moss shelters microscopic, one-celled *diatoms*, which feed insects and invertebrates like the tiny, shrimplike Gammarus. These invertebrates were planted in the river to help the introduced trout, which love cold, clear water where they can hunt by sight. They gobble up Gammarus and black fly larvae, which cover rocks in clear, fast-moving water. All of which helps explain why the native fish have mostly disappeared. They cannot spawn in the cold water, and their young spawned on the tributaries cannot escape the hungry trout, carp, and catfish.

Other changes rippled through the ecosystem with the change in the river. For instance, elimination of the floods proved a boon for the resourceful salt cedar, also known as tamarisk. These thirsty, fast-growing imports quickly colonized the new, fluctuating waterline. The tamarisks exude chemicals that drive out other plants, root readily from debris washed downstream, and choke off the competition. Along most of the 277-mile (445 km) length of the canyon, the tamarisk have moved into the niche that might otherwise have gone to some combination of willows and cottonwoods.

The tamarisk invasion in its turn created a long list of winners and losers. Some suffered, including the willow-loving flycatchers, the mud-loving swallows, and the cattail-loving yellowthroats. Others thrived—beetles, cicadas, and some birds. Most spectacular are the bald eagles, which flock to Nankoweap Creek in growing numbers each winter to eat their fill of the rainbow trout spawning in frenzied, mindless passion. The eagles probably didn't make much use of the canyon before the dam since they would have had a hard time finding fish in the opaque waters. Peregrine falcons also appear to be doing well, since the canyon apparently boasts the largest known population of the world's fastest fliers. They patrol the canyons, preying on the abundant swifts and bats, which in turn prey on the plentiful insects spawned by the enhanced productivity of the water and the streamside vegetation. Other birds have expanded their ranges into the canyon, moving along the ecological highway of the streamside vegetation, including sparrows, starlings, black-chinned hummingbirds, summer tanagers, hooded orioles, yellow warblers, and great-tailed grackles.

GRAND CANYON REVEALS THE HISTORY OF THE EARTH

The great gash of the Grand Canyon also provides perhaps the single most dramatic lesson in geology and the Earth's history on the planet.

The Colorado River cut down through the leading edge of the uplifted Colorado Plateau in the past five million years as the same forces that created the Basin and Range Province uplifted the Rocky Mountains. The 1,400-mile-long (2,253 km) Colorado River carries only a fraction of the water that flows down the Mississippi, but since its gradient is 10 times as steep it erodes far more rock and dirt. The Grand Canyon lies on a 277-mile (445.79 km) stretch of the Colorado River that starts in the Rocky Mountains and flows all the way to the Gulf of California.

Erosion carved away thousands of feet of sediment as the canyon rose, so that the youngest of the sedimentary layers along the top of the Grand Canyon are about 260 million years old. The river recently has carried away everything laid down earlier than that. The youngest formation at the canyon rim is Kaibab Limestone, made of the compressed skeletons of microscopic creatures living in a shallow sea covering what is now the western United States. The oldest rocks in the Grand Canyon are more than a mile below in the inner gorge, where they are so hard and unyielding that they have produced some of the world's most impressive rapids. Those Precambrian rocks date back nearly 2 billion years and include Elves Chasm gneiss, a metamorphic rock formed under great pressure far beneath the surface and then thrust upward until exposed by the Colorado River.

That means that the Grand Canyon lays out the detailed geological history of the Earth between 2 billion and 250 million years ago, nearly halfway back to its origins. Most of the rocks exposed in the towering walls of the canyon are sedimentary, laid down in the bottom of an endless succession of shallow seas and deep lakes. Some layers mark times when the land rose, the seas fell, and vast fields of sand dunes that dwarf the Sahara left their traces (as can be seen in the color insert on page C-2). Some of the layers mark times when Earth shifted and erupted, leaving great layers of lava. One of the biggest rapids in the bottom of the Grand Canyon marks the place where a flood of lava blocked the Colorado River, creating a deep lake that eventually overtopped the lava dam and roared downstream in a devastating flood.

The geological record in the walls of the Grand Canyon for that 2-billion-year swath of time isn't quite complete. Some periods are completely missing, including the so-called Great Unconformity, which consists of all the sediments laid down between about 500 million and 400 million years ago. This means that during that period the continent was rising, as it is now. All the rocks laid down before were stripped away by erosion, before the uplift stopped and new layers of rock were deposited once again. Aside from these gaps, the Grand Canyon represents one of the most complete records of the geologic history of Earth.

✧3 ✧✧✧✧✧✧✧✧✧✧✧✧✧✧✧✧✧✧✧✧✧✧✧✧✧✧✧

Great Basin Desert

Utah, Arizona, Nevada

The sprawling Great Basin Desert gives North America a cold, interior *rain shadow desert* to rival Asia's Gobi Desert. Haunted by the harsh winters of its 6,000–7,000-foot (2,000–2,333 m) elevation, screened from rain by the towering Sierra Nevadas and California to the west and the Rocky Mountains to the east, the Great Basin's endless mountain chains, massive salt flats, fossil lakebeds, and rolling expanses of sagebrush present a harsh, dramatic, often monochromatic landscape that challenges the plants, animals, and people who venture into its soul-stirring expanse.

The Great Basin Desert encompasses more than 190,000 square miles (492,000 sq km), filling the space between the Wasatch Mountains on the east, the Columbia Plateau on the north, the Mojave Desert to the southwest, and the massive uplift of the Mogollon Rim to the south in Arizona. Many experts also include as a division of the Great Basin Desert the lower-elevation Painted Desert and Monument Valley in Arizona. This neatly divides the Great Basin Desert into two major habitats—the rolling, mountain-punctuated, sagebrush-dominated expanses to the north and east and the dramatic, colorful, layered expanses of the Painted Desert and Monument Valley and portions of the Grand Canyon at the southern edge.

GREAT BASIN: TERRIBLE THIRST AND ENDLESS SAGEBRUSH

The same forces that stretched, pulled, and uplifted the entire American Southwest also created the landscape of the Great Basin Desert, a portion of the larger Basin and Range Province, which extends from California's Sierra Nevadas down into Mexico and Texas and up to Nevada and Utah. One old survey map described the mostly north-south running mountain chains of this area as giant caterpillars, crawling haphazardly northward. The mountains rise to about 9,000 feet from the mostly flat, low-lying, down-dropped blocks of intervening desert, which lie at an elevation of

This reflective arm of Lake Powell represents one of the most massive, vital, and controversial engineering projects in human history, the construction of a chain of reservoirs along the Colorado River that now provides irrigation and drinking water to people in seven states and has made possible the development of major cities in the midst of the desert. However, environmentalists insist much of the water is lost through seepage and evaporation or wasted on thirsty, government-subsidized plants like cotton. *(Peter Aleshire)*

1,000 to 6,000 feet (333 to 2,000 m). Most of the mountain ranges are about 60 to 120 miles (96–192 km) long and perhaps 3 to 15 miles (5–24 km) wide.

Ecologist Ann Zwinger wrote a vivid account of the appearance of this vast desert in her book *The Mysterious Lands.* "The Great Basin Desert has a past-finished aspect, as if all that could be done to it has been done, and now it is old and tired and worn out, grizzled and gutted, faded and weather beaten. Sometimes the land has a worn, velvet look, tucked with arroyos, pleated with mountains, a landscape seemingly without seasons or eternally half past autumn, a landscape left out to dry, forgotten, tattered with rain, wrinkled with sun, and yet, in a peculiar sense I cannot explain, always vital and never forlorn."

Cut off from the wet storms generated over the ocean by ranges of mountains, the Great Basin is a rain shadow desert. Most areas get just

6 to 12 inches (152–304 mm) of rain annually. Worse yet, 60 percent of that moisture comes during the cold, frost-prone, snow-dusted winters, when it can do plants and animals the least good. Moreover, the region forms a great, thirsty bowl in which almost all of the rivers and streams start in scattered, rugged mountaintops and run down to deep low points, with no exterior drainage. Therefore, the streams tend to gush during the short and unreliable wet months to collect in low-lying depressions, which once harbored great ice age lakes, but which have now turned into salt flats, made sterile by the salt and minerals left behind by the evaporation of first those giant ice age lakes and now by these fleeting, seasonal lakes. (The salt flats can be seen in the color insert on page C-8.) Most of the drainage ends up in the Humboldt Sink, which includes the saltier than seawater Great Salt Lake, an incongruous shimmer that is but a pathetic remnant of an ice age lake that once constituted a virtual inland sea.

This whole stretched, austere linear landscape was created in the tugging and pulling that took place as the western half of North America was altered in the titanic jostling of plate tectonics. The long, slow-motion collision between the North American Plate and the Pacific Plate forced the edge of the North American Plate down beneath the larger, denser edge of the Pacific Plate. The leading edge of the North American Plate melted at 50 to 100 miles (80–160 km) beneath the surface, and some of the molten rock escaped back to the surface along fractures in the overlying rock, creating chains of volcanoes like the present-day Cascade Range along the Pacific Northwest. Meanwhile, the conveyor belt movement of the Pacific Plate smashed a series of massive islands and fragments of other continents onto the western edge of the Pacific Plate, adding California and the towering Sierra Nevadas to the western edge of the Great Basin. This towering mountain range blocked moisture from the ocean and set the stage for the current landscape and climate.

At some point, a shift in the currents in the deep mantle driving the two crustal plates together shifted, transforming the head-on collision into a massive system of transverse faults that include the infamous San Andreas. This opened up the Gulf of California, put pressure on the San Andreas Fault, and created the north-south mountain chains of North American deserts. Pressure from below pushed up blocks of the crust along fault lines while dropping the intervening valleys.

The landscape remains in turmoil. In many places, fresh faults cut across lava flows dating back 30 million years. Earthquakes often jiggle the mountain ranges and create fresh fault lines, although not nearly as frequently as to the west in California along the San Andreas Fault.

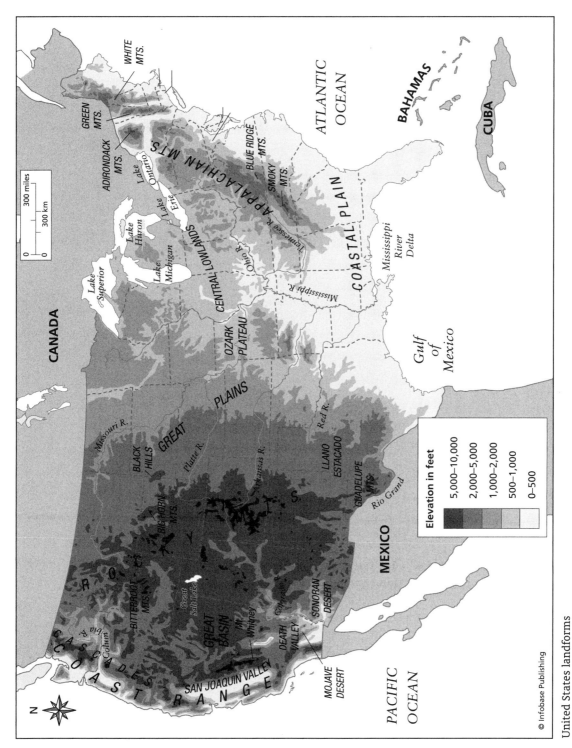

WHITE MTS.

GREEN MTS.

ADIRONDACK MTS.

BLUE RIDGE MTS.

SMOKY MTS.

APPALACHIAN MTS.

Tennessee R.

COASTAL PLAIN

ATLANTIC OCEAN

BAHAMAS

CUBA

Lake Ontario

Lake Erie

Lake Huron

Lake Michigan

Lake Superior

CENTRAL LOWLANDS

Ohio R.

Mississippi River Delta

CANADA

Mississippi R.

OZARK PLATEAU

Gulf of Mexico

GREAT PLAINS

Missouri R.

BLACK HILLS

Platte R.

Arkansas R.

Red R.

LLANO ESTACADO

GUADELUPE MTS.

Rio Grand

Elevation in feet

| 5,000–10,000 |
| 2,000–5,000 |
| 1,000–2,000 |
| 500–1,000 |
| 0–500 |

BIG HORN MTS.

ROCKY MTS.

BITTERROOT MTS.

Great Salt Lake

GREAT BASIN

Mt. Whitney

DEATH VALLEY

Colorado R.

SONORAN DESERT

MEXICO

Columbia R.

CASCADES

COAST RANGE

SAN JOAQUIN VALLEY

MOJAVE DESERT

PACIFIC OCEAN

300 miles

300 km

N

© Infobase Publishing

United States landforms

The colorful, barren, swirled sands of the Painted Desert mark the boundary between the Great Basin Desert and the warmer, wetter, more diverse Sonoran Desert. Composed of layers of fossilized sea bottom and dune deposits, the easily eroded, mineral-rich Painted Desert harbors treasures like the fossil-rich formations of the Petrified Forest National Monument. *(Peter Aleshire)*

CATACLYSM LEAVES WEALTH OF MINERALS

That complex geological history has left the region with a wealth of minerals, many of them formed when the rocks in these desert ranges were deep beneath the ocean along the crack in the Earth between two crustal plates. The weak crust along such gigantic fissures lets molten rock from the deep Earth escape to the surface, as it does now along undersea ridges like the Mid-Atlantic Ridge, which is recognized as the greatest mountain chain on Earth. As magma and superheated water percolates through such fractures in the crust, the heat and pressure spur chemical reactions that cause a variety of minerals to form in the fissures. So the gold, copper, silver, iron, *lithium*, beryllium, molybdenum, and barite that have drawn miners to the Great Basin Desert for more than a century all bear witness to the complex and violent geological history of the rocks that comprise its mountains.

For most of its history, the Great Basin Desert was a grassland graced by vast lakes that supported thriving populations of hunters and gathers, stalking great herds of antelope, camels, and even mammoths. Some 12,000 years ago during the last Ice Age, places like the now-desolate Carson Sink harbored huge lakes. Flush with more than 18 inches of rainfall a year during that long cold snap in the planet's climate, the once year-round Humboldt River flowed into Lake Lahontan, which flooded most of central and northwestern Nevada. It covered 9,000 square miles (2,330 sq km) and had a high-water mark of 4,378 feet (1,459 m) above sea level.

As the climate warmed and the river withered, it became a fitful and capricious drainage system that mostly vanished into thirsty sands and salt flats. Mark Twain observed that "one of the pleasantest and most invigorating exercises one can contrive is to run and jump across the Humboldt River till he is overheated, and then drink it dry."

The once-mighty Lake Bonneville in Utah formed an even more impressive body of water during those wet, lush times. Trapped in an interior basin, the lake gradually filled up, reaching a high-water mark roughly 14,000 years ago. At that point, it rose above a natural dam of rock at Red Rock Pass in southern Idaho and rushed down to the Snake River. It spawned a flood of biblical proportions. The lake fell 10 feet (3.3 m) in four days. In six weeks, the lake level fell 350 feet (117 m), causing a massive flood rushing down into the Snake River, whose traces remain vivid and jumbled all along that path. The lake stabilized at about 4,800 feet (1,600 m) above sea level for the next 6,000 years, before climate shift gradually dried it up.

The Great Salt Lake is another remnant of the Ice Age. As it evaporated, it left behind salts and minerals. That resulted in the Bonneville Salt Flats, a place so hard packed and flat with crystallized salts that rocket-powered race cars now use it to set land speed records.

The Great Basin didn't actually become a desert until after the ancient lake vanished and the climate warmed, which means the plants and animals have perfected their elaborate adaptations to a desert environment in the past 6,000 to 10,000 years.

A LETHAL BARRIER TO EXPLORATION

For much of the nation's history, the Great Basin Desert formed a terrible barrier to explorers and settlers, especially after the discovery of gold in California in 1848 spurred the California gold rush. Legendary explorer Jedediah Smith made the first recorded crossing of the basin in 1824, although he left no documentation of his route or the things he saw. John C. Fremont mapped a chunk of the eastern desert in 1846, but didn't try to cross its flat, waterless expanse. It was the desperation of the gold seekers in 1848 that prompted the first official government survey of the basin in 1867–68.

The Great Basin's Carson Sink and the Humboldt Sink posed the most dangerous obstacles to the crossing of the continent for settlers and gold rushers. Both required the slow-moving wagon trains to cover 40 miles (64 km) or more between water holes, often in conditions that slowed travel to a crawl. The Carson Sink is a 5,000-square-mile (13,000-sq-km) stretch of the Nevada desert in the pitiless rain shadow of the Sierra Madre. Its six inches of rain a year come in cloudbursts that gouge out channels in the dry landscape, since few plants exist to slow erosion. When it does rain, the water pools in the low points and dissolves the salts left by vanished Ice Age lakes, creating a saline sludge that could poison livestock and even kill migrating waterbirds that stopped to rest.

Mark Twain noted the trail was "white with the bones of oxen and horses. It would hardly be an exaggeration to say that we could have walked the 40 miles and set our feet on a bone on every step."

Bennett Clark crossed the Carson Sink and left a vivid account. "We found water in holes . . . dug by those before us. It was cool but most horrible to taste—a mixture of alkali and sulfur and no doubt all coming from the sink. Taking the general aspect of this desert into view, and the fact that there is an absence of every thing desirable and an abundance of every thing pernicious here coupled with what we saw, we cannot conceive a hill more full of horrors. It realizes all that such a mind as Dante's could imagine."

A SAGEBRUSH REALM

Despite the hardships the desert imposed on travelers, the plants and animals that evolved to fit into its austere seasons and angular design demonstrate the adaptability of life, especially in the most unlikely places. The transition from the low, hot Sonoran Desert to the high, cold Great Basin Desert demonstrates the tradeoffs that plants and animals must make in response to conditions. The Sonoran Desert's saguaro can withstand months without rain, but cannot withstand frost and relies on summer monsoon rain. The frost-resistant Joshua tree of the Mojave Desert shrugs off temperatures that would kill a saguaro, but could not withstand the heat and intermittent droughts of the Sonoran. The creosote bush that so stubbornly resists heat and drought gives way to sagebrush in the face of freezing winters. The transition from the heat-adapted Mojave to the cold-adapted Great Basin Desert starts when the inconspicuous Blackbrush displaces the creosote. The Blackbrush, in turn, soon mingles with the sagebrush, the fragrant, tough, cold-adapted signature plant of the northern reaches of the Great Basin Desert.

Ecologist Ann Zwinger observed, "Boundaries like this one fascinate me. Where does the last saguaro become a mere armless post in the ground and finally give up its footing? Where does the kangaroo rat pause, one well-adapted desert foot poised in the air, nose twitching toward a wetter, lusher existence, and not cross over? Where is the line beyond which the desert cockroach does not tunnel? Where is the barrier that keeps the sidewinder and the fringe-toed lizard at home on the hot sands? Where does the desert tortoise blink its slow eyes and turn back to the only home it knows? In trying to define where a desert is not, one learns where it is."

The great, continuous realm of sagebrush that defines the Great Basin Desert constitutes the single largest range of any ecosystem in the western United States, covering some 300 million acres (1.2 million sq km) and half of 11 western states. The sagebrush *ecosystem* evolved quickly after the planet warmed and the glaciers retreated some 12,000 years ago. Gray-green, fragrant, and stubborn, the leaves of the sagebrush are covered with almost furry hairs that protect them from both heat and frost. Sagebrush has both a fibrous surface root system for drinking in even fleeting, scattered rains and a deep-reaching taproot to quest down for groundwater. Although sagebrush plains seem flat and easy to travel through, each bush creates its own little mound as it grows up through the sand that drops from the almost ceaseless winds riffling through its leaves. For the wagon trains of settlers in the 1800s, the mounds around the plants made the sagebrush plains a great misery of constant lurching and bumping.

A single, shoulder-high sage may live 150 years. Sage keeps its leaves all year long, weathering both 100-degree summers and freezing winters. It uses a different process for converting sunlight into energy, which makes it slow-growing but stubborn and drought resistant.

Sagebrush did not truly take over the Great Basin Desert until people tried to make a profit from the desert by grazing cattle there. Once, the sagebrush alternated with grasslands over much of the area. But the cattle quickly chomped the grass. Once the grass was gone, the wildfires that used to control the sagebrush no longer had fuel to spread. But the cattle also couldn't control the sagebrush because the leaves have resins to protect against drought that give most animals indigestion. As a result, cattle will mostly not touch it. So after a few decades of eating most of the grass, the cattle grazing in a huge area ran out of things to eat. And because a single bush can spread a million seeds in a year, the sagebrush invaded the overgrazed grasslands, creating a vast monoculture of sagebrush.

ADAPTED TO THE SAGEBRUSH OCEAN

The Great Basin Desert harbors far fewer species than the warm, summer-rain-blessed Sonoran Desert to the south. Only a handful of flowers like the plains daisy and the yellow parsley bloom in the spring. Only a handful of birds, notably the horned lark, flit through its expanses. Horned larks account for almost all the flocks of birds winging through the sagebrush. They build their nests on the ground, a necessity here because not a single tree rises from this great sagebrush ocean for miles at a stretch. Some populations of horned larks build a crude nest on the ground, carefully putting pebbles or mud pellets to one side to create a flat, smoothly fitted pavement, for reasons that mystify biologists. Perhaps it is some odd takeoff on other populations of horned larks who build little walls of such pebbles, which appear to function as a windbreak.

The chilled soil lacks the organic debris and nutrients that normally fuel plant growth. Fortunately, the struggling plants of the Great Basin get help from mosses and *lichens*, which grow on their roots and create a spidery network of connections in the soil. The lichens put out threads that bind to the bits of dirt in the soil. The treaded filaments knit together the soil, which reduces erosion by the relentless wind. Other components of alga and fungus that live on the roots draw nutrients from the plants and pay their way by producing free nitrogen, a vital element for plant growth. This microscopic community in the soil is vital for the survival of most plants, which explains why dune buggies, cattle, and anything else that breaks up the soil and snaps these microscopic connections leave scars that persist for decades.

The black-tailed jackrabbit is one of the most important and exquisitely adapted creatures of this sagebrush universe. These jackrabbits inhabit every desert of North America, but are especially important in the harsh conditions of the Great Basin. With a family history that stretches back 20 million years, the jackrabbits love to nibble grass and flowers, but they also have cast-iron digestive systems that can handle even the oils in the leaves of the sagebrush. Even more impressive, they can dine on creosote leaves, which are actually poisonous to most other animals. When it is hot, jackrabbits can cool themselves by circulating blood through ears that account for a fifth of their body length. They can cover 15 feet (5 m) in a bound and reach speeds of 35 miles (56 km) an hour. With eyes mounted on the sides of their heads, they have an almost 360-degree field of vision, which makes it impossible to sneak up on them. They often gather in social groups of 20 or more on moonlit nights, where they court their mates with displays of ecstatic jumping about, complete with sprays of hormone-laced urine. In addition, the jackrabbits unwillingly support the desert's coyotes, hawks, eagles, and other predators.

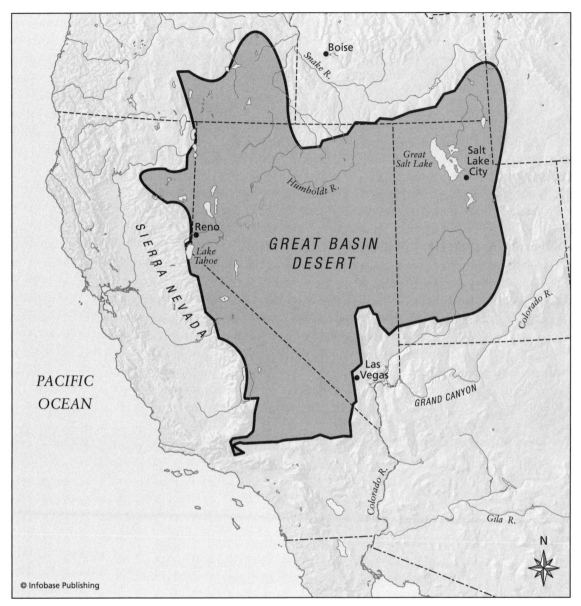

Wind erosion

Another remarkably adapted desert creature is the Great Basin spadefoot toad, an amphibian whose tadpoles must grow up in water in a land with few permanent lakes, rivers, or streams that also freezes every winter. The toads manage this remarkable feat by spending most of their lives buried deep in the dirt, scooping out their burrow by rotating their bodies as they push with first one foot, then the other, and digging with the bony flange of skin on the side of their foot from which they earn their names. While their cousins in warmer deserts may emerge during summer rains to lay their eggs in temporary pools of water, the Great Basin spadefoot toad must rely on scattered, permanent springs. They spend most of the year hidden in their burrows, waiting for warmer weather. They can store water totaling a third of their body weight, sometimes creating a cocoon of mud to reduce water loss through their skin. When awakened by a heavy rain when the air temperature is above 52°F (11°C), the frogs emerge to unleash a deafening chorus to attract a mate. If they are successful, they lay their eggs in the few permanent springs and the eggs hatch and the tadpoles develop with great speed to take advantage of their narrow climatic window of opportunity.

INVADERS UNHINGE AN ECOSYSTEM

Ironically, an exotic grass introduced by human beings now threatens the sagebrush *ecosystem* that expanded so dramatically as a result of human beings and their cattle. The sagebrush populations exploded after overgrazing removed the cold-adapted native grasses. Those grasses used to carry periodic, low-intensity fires that would burn up encroaching brushes. The grass, on the other hand, usually came back quickly after a fire, taking advantage of the nutrients the fire scattered across the soil in the form of ashes. But once the cattle ate most of the grass and eliminated the brushfires, the sagebrush occupied millions of acres of former grassland.

Then, in about 1900, ranchers introduced an Asian grass called cheatgrass, which sprouts in the fall and produces a huge number of seeds. By June, the portion of the grass above the ground dies, providing a ready host for fire. When lightning or human-caused fires ignite the cheatgrass, the flames spread rapidly and kill the sagebrush without hurting the dormant grass roots. The grass sprouts back from the roots and eventually forms dense stands that crowd out almost all other plants. Unfortunately, few of the native animals and insects are adapted to the cheatgrass, which has only a brief growing season when deer, cattle, pronghorns, rodents, and birds like chukars and partridges can digest it. Once the cheatgrass puts out seeds that are covered in a sharp, barbed coat, hardly any animals can eat it.

PAINTED DESERT: COLD WINDS AND BURIED DINOSAURS

Many experts consider the sprawl of colorful high-elevation desert in the northeast corner of Arizona to be a part of the higher, colder Great Basin Desert to the north. The Painted Desert is far from the moist storms of

The Navajo sandstone shown here near Window Rock on the Navajo Reservation in Arizona readily erodes into distinctive shapes, complete with arches and windows—openings that have flaked and grown through solid rock walls as a result of the action of rain and frost. *(Peter Aleshire)*

either the distant Pacific or the Gulf of California. The deluge of summer storms that make the Sonoran Desert one of the richest in the world do not as reliably reach the Painted Desert. Its higher elevation makes the region subject to winter snows and frost, which makes it ecologically more like the Great Basin than either the Mojave or Sonoran.

The Painted Desert is made of an eroded, multicolored rock layer called the Chinle Formation, laid down in a swampy, inland area some 225 million years ago during the Late Triassic period. The layers and the treasure trove of fossils they contain are best seen at the Petrified Forest National Monument.

With only a scattering of bushes that can stand the combination of low rainfall, hot summers, and chilly winters, the landscape of the Painted Desert looks like a scene from another planet. Minerals have tinted the *sedimentary* layers red, brown, purple, and sometimes green. The soft,

CONDORS MAKE A COMEBACK

The rock-climbing biologists dangling in front of the cliff-face condor cave expected the worst, but hoped for the best. They wanted to know why condor 119 and condor 122 had abandoned their nest in the ancient cave in the inaccessible heart of the Grand Canyon. The devoted condor couple was among 34 California condors reared in captivity who were floating on their nine-foot (2.7 m) wingspan across northern Arizona as part of a $25 million effort to avert the extinction of the largest bird in North America.

Condors soared across much of North America 10,000 years ago, feeding on the Ice Age carcasses of mammoths and giant ground sloths. But the last condor was sighted in Arizona in 1924, and by 1983 biologists were forced to gather up the last 22 birds in California. Since then, a captive breeding program has enabled biologists to establish one flock in Arizona, two flocks in California, and one more in Mexico.

Biologists hoped that condors 119 and 122 would be the first of the flock to actually raise chicks in a cave in the Grand Canyon so inaccessible the rock-climbing biologists took a helicopter to get to the cliff top above the nest. Inside, they discovered shards of condor eggshells among the regurgitated hairballs and pellets of the nesting adults. That was discouraging, but they were also electrified to discover condor bones in the back of the cave dating back to the Ice Age. Clearly the condors had come home.

Since then several condor couples have successfully fledged chicks, which means that the expensive reintroduction effort may succeed in returning the lordly scavengers to the skies of the Mojave, Great Basin, and Sonoran Deserts.

Giant vultures that live entirely on carrion, condors once seemed doomed to extinction by the destruction of the great herds of North America, the spread of human settlements, and especially the effect of the pesticide DDT, which thinned their eggshells as it did the shells of bald eagles.

The reintroduction effort has faced odd challenges. The first flock released in California behaved like a youth gang. They flocked to a country club golf course, where they sat around watching people around the barbecue pits, making buzzard comments among themselves. Some took to attacking cars in the parking lot and ripping off the windshield wipers. "It was like *Lord of the Flies,*" observed one biologist. More important, in the first year about 20 percent of the released birds died, mostly as a result of encounters with power poles and human beings. The next batch of birds was reared with hand puppets so they would not get used to people, and fake power lines were put in the birds' enclosures, which delivered a mild electric shock if landed upon. Occasionally a human being would stand at a distance from the enclosure. Once the birds were all focused on the distant human figure, keepers would rush suddenly out of hiding, shouting and stamping to instill fear of human beings.

The new conditioning paid off when biologists again released condors into the wild. The biggest setback came when five condors died of lead poisoning after feeding on a bullet-riddled carcass. Three condors have been shot by random hunters. One condor was killed by a golden eagle. Coyotes have claimed several others, mostly foolish young condors who spent the night on the ground. But gradually the condors have acquired the survival skills that they would have learned from their wild parents. Ambitious individuals have ventured north 200 miles or more, looking for carrion in Utah. Many have taken to showing up at the heavily populated south rim of the Grand Canyon. The appearance of condors inevitably draws exclamations from tourists, but condor minders working for the reintroduction effort soon show up to chase them away.

The recent birth of a chick in the wild has infused biologists with new hope after years of effort. Finally a new generation of condors seems ready to launch themselves from the same caves that sheltered their ancestors more than 10,000 years ago.

The spires of sandstone define the southern reaches of the Great Basin Desert, which covers most of Utah and Nevada and extends into northern Arizona. These formations on the Navajo Reservation in northeastern Arizona make this area one of the most iconic of all desert landscapes. *(Peter Aleshire)*

crumbling, rounded landscape seems hollowed and sculpted by wind and rain, a weary, ancient landscape redeemed by its lurid colors.

In the Petrified Forest National Monument, this already surreal landscape is pushed toward fantasy by a profusion of fossils, including a whole forest of trees that have been turned to brightly colored stone. Trees buried in saturated mud were cut off from oxygen, which means that bacteria could not consume them. Instead, the trees were buried under a deepening weight of sediment. Time and pressure allowed mineral-laden water to seep into the matrix of wood, eventually fossilizing it with a mingling of brightly colored minerals and jewel-like crystals.

This same process also preserved the bones of many of the creatures that lived more than 200 million years ago, at the dawn of the age of dinosaurs. The fossil experts working at the Petrified Forest find one or two new species every year, casting new light on old theories about many creatures. For instance, one recent discovery of a small relative of modern crocodiles casts doubt on existing theories of how dinosaurs developed. Previous discoveries of the fossilized teeth of this ancient crocodile, *Revueltosaurus callenderi*, led experts to believe that it was the ancestor of the plant-eating dinosaurs such as stegosaurus and triceratops, two of the best-known examples of the dinosaurs that dominated the planet's living things until some 65 million years ago. At that point, most experts believe the impact of a giant meteorite caused a dust cloud that caused the extinction of the great majority of living species, including all the dinosaurs. The recent find in the Petrified Forest demonstrated that this alligatorlike swamp-dwelling hunter was not related to the dinosaurs after all. Instead, the bones suggest this supposed dinosaur that lived more than 200 million years ago was a relative of modern crocodiles. *Revueltosaurus* was about four feet long, with a rounded skull and legs less slung to the side than modern crocodiles. Twin strips of armor plating down its back protected it. The find proves that the dominant plant-eating dinosaurs like the triceratops may have emerged about 25 million years later

THE "BLUEBERRIES" THAT PREDICTED AN OCEAN

The Great Basin Desert harbors enigmatic sandstone marbles that have already helped prove that Mars once had oceans. The geological mystery story starts on the Red Planet, where the robot rover *Opportunity* went trundling across the surface looking for signs of water and beamed back to Earth images of perplexing stone nodules, perfectly round rocks the size of blueberries scattered across the rust-red Martian surface in the equatorial plain of Meridiani Planum.

Geologists were puzzled until they discovered that University of Utah researcher Marjorie Chan predicted *Opportunity* would find those "blueberries" after she spent eight years studying similar stones in southern Utah.

Spacecraft orbiting Mars had previously detected surface deposits of hematite, a form of iron that on Earth forms only in water. Chan's enigmatic stone nodules in Utah also proved rich in hematite. She concluded these concretions precipitated out of iron-rich water inside layers of saturated sandstone and grew into perfect spheres as they dissolved a little niche in the surrounding rock. On Mars, the sedimentary rock matrix for the blueberries was made of finely crushed layers of volcanic rock.

than the experts thought. So they did not arise at the same time as the meat-eating ancestors of the tyrannosaurus, which modifies the scientific understanding of the dinosaurs' family tree. The discovery demonstrates the importance of deserts in reconstructing the history of the Earth and its inhabitants. The barren, easily eroded desert soils easily yield up their secrets, which explains why most of the fossils that have enabled scientists to reconstruct human evolution, mass extinctions, and the shifts of evolution have been found in desert regions like the Petrified Forest in the Painted Desert.

4

Chihuahuan Desert
Arizona, Texas, Mexico

The same forces that have shaped the other North American deserts by creating the geologically stretched *Basin and Range* Province also forged the 280,000-square-mile (450,616 sq km) Chihuahuan Desert. This great desert plain punctuated with a patterned scattering of north-south trending mountains starts in the shadow of the massive Sierra Madre in Mexico, runs north into Texas and New Mexico, and finally into the southeastern corner of Arizona.

A rain shadow desert of summer storms and winter droughts, the Chihuahuan Desert harbors remarkably well-adapted creatures, tenacious plants dominated by yuccas (as shown in the color insert on page C-4), and geological marvels like the limestone Carlsbad Caverns, the blinding *gypsum* sand dunes of White Sands, and the meanders of the Rio Grande River.

The Chihuahuan neatly rounds out the climatic range of North American deserts. It is the largest and highest on average, with an average elevation of 4,000 feet (1,219 m). It also lies deep in the rain shadow of the massive Sierra Madre range, a jagged wilderness of tormented rock created by the uplift of continental collisions that started 65 million years ago as the supercontinent of Pangea gradually broke up and scattered across the globe, propelled by the constant movement of tectonic plates. Those same forces built the Rocky Mountains farther north and ultimately pasted onto the leading edge of North America the areas that now comprise California, Washington, and Oregon. The towering Sierra Madre cut off most winter rains in the Chihuahuan Desert, so the region's 8–14 inches (203–355 mm) of rainfall come almost entirely in the summer. The long, hot dry season in the Chihuahuan stretches from October to early June. That neatly reverses the rainfall pattern in the cold Great Basin Desert, with its freezing winter rains and snow. As a result, the Chihuahuan has a greater diversity of plants and wildlife than the Great Basin, but far less than the Sonoran, which has alternating winter and summer rains.

The effects of the Sierra Madre on climate largely account for the presence of the Chihuahuan Desert. Wet storms sweeping in from the Gulf of California and the Pacific Ocean break against the western flank of those stone ramparts, which wring out the moisture as clouds rise into the colder, higher altitudes or deflect storms northwest into the Sonoran Desert. On the east side of the 13,000-foot-tall (3,962 m) Sierra Madre, chilled, dry air flows down into the Chihuahuan's desert basins, gaining enough energy from compression as it drops to heat up by about 4 degrees for every 1,000 feet (304 m). The resulting hot, dry winds sustain this unique desert.

Much closer to the equator than the other North American deserts, the clear, dry air of the Chihuahuan offers little resistance to the Sun's rays. The ground heats up quickly in the daytime, since 90 to 95 percent of the Sun's energy reaches the ground. By contrast, clouds and haze in the form of water vapor typically block half the Sun's energy in more humid places. That same lack of moisture in the desert air allows the infrared heat radiating off the ground at night to escape quickly back into the atmosphere. As a result, the Chihuahuan Desert typically has hot days and cold nights, with temperature swings of 45 degrees in a single day.

The uneven rainfall combined with the cold winters restrict the plant life of the Chihuahuan Desert, so it lacks the signature Joshua tree of the

THE MYSTERY OF THE CATACLYSM

Some 37 million years ago as the Basin and Range Province took shape, a long, violent series of volcanic eruptions shaped the face of the Big Bend area and much of the rest of the Chihuahuan Desert. This period of intense volcanic activity shaped much of the American Southwest. In some places, great bubbles of molten rock pushed toward the surface, remelting rocks and causing great domes, bows, and folds. In many places, the superheated, pressurized rock broke through to the surface, creating volcanoes, lava flows, and outbursts of ash that sometimes smothered large areas. This period of volcanic activity left many of the distinctive landforms of the Southwest, including badlands covered with jagged lava and volcanic plugs, monoliths of once-molten rock that hardened in the throat of a volcano. These volcanic plugs now loom over an eroded landscape of softer rock.

For a long time, geologists believed that the Earth was patient and steady in its shifts and that change took place at a steady pace. Increasingly, however, geologists have come to recognize that the deep currents in the Earth's semi-molten *mantle* must undergo great changes or cycles that sometimes cause a global increase in volcanic activity. These periods of increased volcanic activity may account for dramatic transformations in Earth's surface like the breakup of the Pangea supercontinent, climatic shifts, and the shape of the North American Southwest and its deserts. For whatever reason, the major volcanic activity in the Chihuahuan largely ended about 35 million years ago. Since then, erosion has dominated throughout the region as time, ice, and water set to work leveling both the Rocky Mountains and the Sierra Madre.

Mojave or the frost-sensitive saguaro of the Sonoran. On the other hand, it has more variety in plant life than the sagebrush plains of the Great Basin. Varieties of yucca and century plant are the defining plants of the Chihuahuan Desert. (Another example of plant life can be seen on the color insert on page C-4.)

CENTURY PLANT GROWS FATALLY TALL TO SURVIVE

The massive century plant is one of the most distinctive plants of the Chihuahuan, a tough, sharp-spined member of the lily family with a dramatic strategy for spreading its seeds. One of the largest agaves, the century plant may persist for 50 years before it reproduces in a single season of fatal extravagance. Normally, the century plant gathers energy through its broad leaves that end in a wicked point. The leaf rosette at the base eventually reaches two or three feet across, the waxy surface of its leaves hoarding moisture and its tough root gathering up every drop of moisture. A waxy coating of *hydrocarbons* on the huge leaf surface reflects 75 percent of the ultraviolet and near-infrared heat radiation, which slows evaporation, conserves water, and reduces damage when the leaves get dehydrated. After decades of tenacious growth, the century plant will pour all of its energy into growing a single remarkable stalk that can tower 30 feet (9.14 m) above its humble base. The stalk then produces an outpouring of yellow, tubular flowers, creating a strange forest of great stalks that makes a once-inconspicuous hillside bristle with color. Remarkably, the plant puts so much energy into sustaining this single, outlandish flowering stalk that it dies with the fading of the blossoms.

Biologists believe this showy, high-risk reproductive strategy is linked directly to the migrations of bats, the major pollinators of the agave. Biologists note that the agave flowers often smell faintly of rotten meat, which attracts not only many of the small desert flies but also bats. The scent of the flowers peaks between eight and 10 at night, precisely when the nectar-feeding bats are most active. Moreover, the precise mix of nutrients and the design of the flowers seem perfectly adapted to the bats' needs. It also makes sense that a plant trying to attract the attention of night-flying bats would put the sweet bait of the nectar on a tall stalk easily visible in the darkness and easily accessible for bats that lack the dexterity of a bee or a hummingbird.

A TALE OF HUNGRY BATS AND LUSH FLOWERS

Gary Paul Nabhan and Stephen L. Buchmann in *The Forgotten Pollinators* detail the remarkable relationship between the bats and the agave.

Nectar-feeders like the long-nose bats travel a looping 3,200-mile (5,150 km) migratory route every year that appears precisely timed to take them from wintering caves deep in Mexico to caves in which they raise their young as far north as Tucson, Arizona, and Big Bend, Texas. The migratory route is timed to take advantage of the flowering of 16 different plant species, including tree morning glories, century plants, and saguaros.

Sadly, the bats have been battered by the loss of roosting sites in both Mexico and the United States, as well as the effects of pesticides and other hazards. Caves that once harbored millions of bats are now empty, and some of the migratory bats have dwindled to threatened status. As a result, biologists have noted a decline in the plants the bats pollinate, including the agave and the saguaro.

The agave and its cousins have also long sustained human beings. Native Americans quickly discovered that the agave offers a treasure trove of nutrition if they are harvested just before the plants pour that hoarded energy into growing the 30-foot-tall (9.1 m) stalk. Many Native American cultures hacked out the rich heart of the plant or the young stalk, then roasted the great mass in rock-lined pits. From the sweet, pulpy heart they would make a nutritious, high-energy snack that would last for months when dried. They also made an alcoholic beverage. Today, the agave are still used to make mescal and tequila, but the popularity of these alcoholic beverages has resulted in a worrisome overharvesting of agave in Mexico, with an estimated 1 million plants a year chopped down to make bootleg liquor in Sonora, Mexico, alone.

The agave come in many varieties in the Chihuahuan Desert, including the lechuguilla, commonly referred to as the shin dagger. The leaves of this small plant roll at the tips into a finger-length needle filled with sap that contains a strong muscle contractor that makes the wicked wounds it inflicts especially painful. The lechuguilla, which puts out flowering stalks every 25 to 35 years, can also reproduce by sprouting from rootlets. As a result, a whole hillside of stalks may spring from a single plant. Another common plant is the sotol, a normally slow-growing plant that puts out a stalk that spurts upward by a foot a day after 12 or 15 years. It also yields a rich food source from a heart about the size of a cabbage and can also be used to make a sweet, alcoholic drink.

The high altitude, cold winters, and dry summers have impoverished the variety of cactus in the Chihuahuan, with the exception of the seemingly indestructible prickly pear, which remains widespread. The prickly pear makes energy from the sun with the *chlorophyll* in its green skin, which allows it to convert its leaves and stems into long spines and hairlike tormenters called glochids. The quick-growing prickly pear stores water in its thick pads and can shrivel in the dry season and swell up at the first rain. Moreover, the cactus has high concentrations of calcium oxalate crystals just under its skin. This prevents evaporation and also makes the pads toxic to most animals.

The prickly pear uses a specialized method of turning the sun's rays into food common to many desert plants. Normally, tree leaves convert the sun's energy into food as the light hits the leaf. However, that requires the plant to open up its pores, which means it loses a lot of moisture. By contrast, cacti (such as the one shown in the color insert on page C-5) and other desert plants use a version of photosynthesis called crassulacean acid metabolism (CAM), which reduces water use by 70 percent. Plants that use CAM open their pores, or stomata, to take in carbon dioxide from the air only at night. Come sunlight, they close their stomatas so they can complete the process of photosynthesis while still sealed up, preventing water loss. The tradeoff is that they cannot make energy from breaking up the carbon dioxide nearly as fast as plants that do take in light and carry out photosynthesis all at one time, which explains why CAM plants like cactus and agave grow much more slowly than plants that don't have to fanatically hoard their moisture.

In nature, no matter how elaborate a plant's defenses, some animal will evolve the ability to break through them. So the thorned, poisonous prickly pear is the mainstay of the collared peccary, a small, bristly relative of swine with wicked teeth, a sensitive, fleshy nose, and an endearing repertoire of grunts used to keep track of each other in thick brush. The peccaries consider prickly pear a delicacy, despite the darning needle spines, the glochids that can blind cattle, and the calcium oxalate crystals that deter almost all other diners. The peccaries manage this feat with tough tongues, thick hides, and heavy-duty kidneys.

CREATURES THAT NEVER TAKE A DRINK

Any creatures living in a desert where eight months without significant rain is routine must have intricate adaptations to these conditions. For instance, the desert pocket mouse can go its whole life without a drink of water. The tiny, big-eyed rodents dig burrows up to five feet deep (1.52 m), usually with at least two entrances the size of a broom handle. Deep beneath the ground they are protected from the heat and cold and enjoy nearly constant conditions with three times the humidity of the desert floor above. That is essential, since they have such a large surface area relative to their weight that they would otherwise have a hard time keeping their body temperature constant. Moreover, they can slip in and out of a hibernation-like state, which dramatically slows their heart rate and metabolic process. They have such efficient kidneys and digestive systems that they can extract all the moisture they need from the seeds, plants, and insects on which they live.

The intelligent and adaptable coyote remains one of the quintessential creatures of the North American deserts who has thrived in spite of efforts to eliminate them. In fact, more coyotes roam the West now than before Europeans arrived, probably because the destruction of wolves over most of North America has freed the coyote from the constraints of their chief competitor. *(Peter Aleshire)*

On the whole, reptiles are better adapted to the desert than are mammals, which accounts for the much richer variety of lizards and snakes in most deserts. Most creatures store energy in the form of fats and *carbohydrates* or directly burn proteins. When proteins, carbohydrates, and fats are converted to energy, the chemical reaction produces waste products of carbon dioxide and water and nitrogen. Mammals get rid of the waste products in urea, which requires urine that consumes a lot of water. Lizards and snakes convert their nitrogen wastes to uric acid, which requires almost no water and gets rid of twice as much nitrogen per unit as the more soluble urea. As a result, reptiles all start off with a waste-disposal system that makes it easier for them to live in the desert.

Moreover, reptiles do not use energy to keep their body temperatures constant. Again, that gives them certain advantages in the desert, where they don't often have to cope with freezing conditions. The temperature of their environment determines reptiles' body temperatures, which is why most reptiles cannot live in areas with long winters. In the desert, they do have to avoid overheating, which they do by hiding in the shade or in burrows during the heat of the day in the warm season. Also, because they cannot cool themselves through sweating, they do not lose much water.

However, evolution can fashion solutions to heat and drought for even creatures that seem completely unsuited to desert life. For instance, the *Rhabdotus* land snail also manages to survive in the Chihuahuan Desert. The snails, with their soft, moist, easily dehydrated flesh, spend almost all their lives buried in the dry, desert soil sealed up in their coiled shells. Buried an inch below the surface, they seal the opening of their shells with a papery flap, relying on the trapped, insulating air to protect them from the heat and the cold. The shell itself reflects about 90 percent of the sunlight that strikes it. Sealed up in its shell, the snail can last for years, waiting for a good rain. When awakened by the drumming of such a rain, they emerge to feed and mate. When they are moving around, they use 45 times as much water as when they are holed up.

BIG BEND NATIONAL MONUMENT: HARD AND HISTORICAL

This 2,865-square-mile (7,420 sq km) region in a bend of the Rio Grande exemplifies the austere terrain and the complex geological history of the lower-elevation areas of the Chihuahuan Desert.

Lying in a great, down-dropped trough, the park features the typical basin and range topography of low flat basins surrounding sharply uplifted, isolated mountain ranges. The landscape is split by faults that have allowed some chunks to drop to form basins while adjacent land has risen to form eroded mountain ranges, all caused by the ongoing thrusts, stretches, uplifts, and drops that dominate the geology all the way from Mexico's Sierra Madre to the Sierra Nevadas, Cascades, and Rocky Mountains. The Rio Grande, the only major river system in a great expanse of New Mexico and Texas, runs down the bottom of one of the rifts caused by that settling between fault systems and its path defines the heart of the Chihuahuan Desert.

The oldest rocks in Big Bend National Monument date back some 500 million years to the Paleozoic era and consist of limestone and sandstone deposited in the bottom of what was then a vast, shallow, warm ocean or inland sea. At that time, almost no plants or animals had colonized the land so all the fossils bear witness to life's origins in the oceans. The billions of years of Earth's history recorded in the rocks before this period were swallowed up by uplift and erosion in this area and throughout most of the Chihuahuan Desert. Some 500 million years ago, the surface of Earth underwent a prolonged period of thrusting, buckling, and uplift, causing the creation of great mountain chains followed by a long period of erosion. This removed most of those older limestones and sandstones, leaving only telltale traces from their fossil clues left behind.

During most of the *Mesozoic* period between 240 million and 63 million years ago, the region was uplifted high above sea level. At this time, most of the continents were joined into a single supercontinent, which provided the warm, reliable conditions in which the dinosaurs emerged to dominate life on land. Dinosaur tracks and fossils bear witness to their presence here, including fossils of pterodactyls with 50-foot (12-m) wingspans, the largest creatures ever to take to the air. The rocks in Big Bend demonstrate that for a period in the Cretaceous a shallow sea engulfed much of what became North America, leaving telltale layers of limestone. That sea eventually receded as the continents rose and the addition of land to the west cut off the region from the oceans.

The current landscape began to take place in the *Cenozoic* period, the Age of Mammals, which started some 65 million years ago as the dinosaurs died out and shifts in the Earth's crust caused the breakup of the supercontinent. The rise of the Rocky Mountains and the Sierra Madre and the emergence of the Basin and Range Province some 30 million years later established both the current drainage including the Rio Grande and the rain shadows that would eventually produce North America's deserts.

The Rio Grande originates in the Rocky Mountains and runs to the Gulf of Mexico, mostly meandering along a broad plain, but sometimes cutting deep gorges.

CARLSBAD CAVERNS NATIONAL PARK: FANTASTIC REALM

One of the most remarkable geological features of the Chihuahuan Desert actually lies far beneath the surface, the Carlsbad Caverns, a vast limestone cave decorated with a fantasy of natural stone shapes. The cavern is the most spectacular and accessible of many such caverns that have formed in the once-sea-bottom layers of limestone that underlie the region.

The story starts 250 million years ago with the drift to the bottom of a warm shallow sea of the calcium-rich remains of often-microscopic sea creatures. As the continent shifted and the sea bottom subsided, the skeletons of these creatures formed layers of mud thousands of feet thick. As the subsidence continued and erosion piled deep layers of calcium-rich mud and sediment on top, the heat and pressure eventually fused the mud layers into limestone.

The restless Earth shifted once again, and the now-fused limestone layers rose again toward the surface, cracked and fractured by the pressure of that fall and rise. Near the surface, rainwater made slightly *acidic* by its passage through the soil seeped into the cracks and fractures of the still-buried layers of limestone. Eventually, pressures from below pushed the limestone layers up toward the water table, the zone at which the rocks are saturated by water percolating down from above. Here, the acidic water seeping down from above ran through the cracks and gradually began to dissolve the calcium carbonate in the limestone along those fractures. Other chemical reactions may have hastened this process, including the creation of sulfuric acid from the mineral pyrite found in the lagoon deposits from which the limestone was formed. This acidic groundwater eventually chewed away at the rock to create the caverns. Some geologists think that perhaps the combination of limestone and sulfuric acid formed gypsum, which eventually decomposed in the sulfur-enriched air of the cavern, causing the cavern to essentially hollow.

Eventually, continued uplift and perhaps climatic shifts caused the formation of the bizarre rock formations for which the caverns are famous. That process started when the water table fell below the level of the cavern, leaving it hollow. At that point, heated, pressurized mineral-rich water seeping along fractures from the surface would drip by drip enter the relatively cool, unpressurized air of the cavern. The sudden change in temperature and pressure caused the minerals held in solution in the water to precipitate from liquid to solid form. This process has created a wild variety of rock formations in the cave, including almost transparent curtains of stone, drip-castle spires, iciclelike stalactites hanging from the ceiling, and spearlike stalagmites bristling up from the floor. Although the cave itself may have started forming some 12 million years ago, most of the breathtaking, colorful formations probably started forming more like 10,000 to 20,000 years ago.

The limestone layer in which the cavern formed was actually a massive reef some 250 million years ago, similar to Australia's Great Barrier Reef. At some point, the increasing saltiness of the shallow sea in which it grew apparently killed the reef-building animals. After the reef stopped growing, it was buried. The burial caused cracks to form, which became the fractures along which the cave would eventually develop.

The caves took shape when this ancient buried reef was uplifted some 12 million years ago beneath the Guadalupe Mountains. The caverns now have three major levels, some close to the surface and some about 3,500 feet (1,067 m) below the surface. Evidence suggests that other, higher levels of the caverns were eroded away as the Guadalupe Mountains rose. The cave's temperature remains at a constant 56°F (13°C). The caverns extend through an area 4,500 feet (1,500 m) long, 2,700 feet (900 m) wide, and 900 feet (300 m) from top to bottom.

WHITE SANDS NATIONAL MONUMENT

The Chihuahuan Desert also harbors another geological marvel, the blinding white dunes of White Sands National Monument in New Mexico. These dunes are made of gypsum left behind by the evaporation of a once-vast Ice Age lake. The gypsum crystals are soft and easily scratched, which means that the tiny crystals reflect the light that strikes them like so many microscopic diamonds. That accounts for the blinding white color of the sand dunes. By contrast, most sand dunes in other deserts are made from crystals of *quartz* or tiny rock fragments, which do not scratch easily and therefore reflect far less light.

This area was once submerged in shallow seas, like the rest of the Chihuahuan. But some 250 million years ago an arm of that inland sea was cut off from the ocean, causing it to slowly evaporate as the Red Sea in Israel is doing today. The sea probably advanced and retreated repeatedly as climate shifts and continental drift caused sea levels to rise and fall. Each time a fresh ocean evaporated from the warm shallows, the water left behind its load of salts and minerals. Eventually, this created layers of gypsum up to 500 feet (150 m) thick.

Some 23 million years ago, fresh shifts in the crust caused the broad Tularosa Valley to fracture and drop between two adjoining, mountain-range-uplifting faults. That exposed rock layers loaded with gypsum from that ancient, vanished sea that gradually eroded out of the surrounding cliffs and mountains and ran down into the low-lying valley in between.

During the last Ice Age, these deposits ended up in Lake Otero, which formed at the low point in the valley floor. When Lake Otero finally evaporated 12,000 years ago, it left behind the fine deposits of gypsum grains. The restless winds driven by the desert's strong thermals soon gathered up the gypsum and created the awe-inspiring dune fields of White Sands. Every spring, winds from the southwest reach the steady, 15-mile-an-hour force necessary to create and sculpt a sand dune.

Here, the wind has created a virtual encyclopedia of sand dunes, all made of the stark white gypsum. In the areas with the strongest wind, the sand forms dome-shaped dunes. In other places, the wind creates crescent-shaped barchan dunes, with horns pointing away from the wind and a downwind slope between the horns much steeper than the gradual, upwind slope. Sometimes barchan dunes form a chain of transverse dunes running across the wind direction that march along at a steady rate as a result of avalanches of sand down the steep slope facing away from the wind. Finally, the dune fields also include U-shaped parabolic dunes that are concave on the windward side, their long arms anchored by vegetation.

These dramatic, constantly shifting dunes host their own unique set of exquisitely adapted creatures. Many of the dune species are white versions of other, more common animals found elsewhere, since evolution would favor the shift to a white color to help creatures blend in with the sand and so survive to pass along their tendency toward white. A notable example is the White Sands swift, a lizard that is pure gypsum white except for a vivid blue throat patch and a light blue stripe on its belly. Coyotes, rabbits, and pocket mice here tend to have lighter coats, a striking example of how quickly evolution helps creatures adapt to their surroundings.

The gypsum dunes create often-surprising conditions. For instance, cottonwoods remain the only trees that grow in the monument, and they grow only on the margins of the dunes. That is because cottonwoods originally evolved to quickly colonize sandbars along desert rivers. As a result, they are fast growing and send strong, quick-growing roots questing out along the surface of the sand. That proved just the right tactic for getting a roothold in the soft, shifting sand of the dunes. The cottonwoods take root in the shallow, low-lying depressions that form in the dunes and grow fast enough to avoid inundation by taking advantage of the way in which the gypsum holds moisture several feet beneath the surface to create a saturated area that the stream-adapted cottonwoods tap into.

CHIRICAHUA MOUNTAINS: BETWEEN TWO DESERTS

Sitting on the northwestern edge of the Chihuahuan Desert, the Chiricahua Mountains mingle cataclysmic geology with a bloody history. The

---

LIVING ON ALGAE'S EFFORTS

In most of the dunes, plants need special adaptations to deal with the gypsum, or calcium carbonate, in the soil. Plants that have evolved special techniques for dealing with such calcium carbonates are called gypsophiles, and the Chihuahuan Desert has more such plants than any other desert.

Fortunately, a variety of algae has also developed mechanisms to handle the minerals in the dune sands. Just beneath the blinding white surface, it forms a green layer that constitutes the true base of the food chain in the strange world of the dune's *ecosystem*. The algae provide the only organic matter in most of the dune field. They also chemically alter the scarce nitrogen they find in a way that makes it useable for other plants and animals. These algae, together with certain bacteria, provide the nutrients the plants growing on the dunes need to survive. Ironically, these desert-dwelling algae are directly related to the blue-green algae that live at certain depths in the ocean. Having adapted to desert sand dunes, the dry, encysted, seedlike cells of the algae can survive for up to 80 years in dry desert soils to resume growth as soon as they get enough water.

The Sonoran Desert has a greater diversity of wildflowers than almost any other habitat in the world, thanks to reliable rains in both the summer and winter. Wildflowers like these Mexican gold poppies in the Superstition Mountains of Arizona cope with the regular desert droughts that can last for years by producing massive crops of seeds that wait in the desert soil for the wet years that come every three to 10 years. *(Peter Aleshire)*

The Grand Canyon demonstrates the dramatic impact of elevation on ecosystems. On a day when snow mantles the rim of the canyon and temperatures plunge below freezing, the temperature at the bottom may top 70°. *(Peter Aleshire)*

The bottom of the Grand Canyon is often 30 or 40 degrees hotter than up among the pine trees on the rim. This creates a ribbon of desert habitat connecting several different types of desert. Construction of the Glen Canyon Dam forced dramatic changes in the ecosystem of the Grand Canyon, eliminating the spring floods and replacing the warm muddy water with clear, cold water off the bottom of Lake Powell. *(Peter Aleshire)*

Sand dunes remain one of the most distinctive desert landforms. Usually comprised of sand from dried-up river deltas or inland lakes or seas, the fierce winds of the desert pile the sand into vivid patterns and shapes. Such deposits of sand in other environments become covered and locked into place by plants, but plants in the desert are too sparse to tie down the dunes. *(Peter Aleshire)*

The dramatic buttes and dunes of Monument Valley on the Navajo Reservation in Arizona have become the iconic desert landscape for many people, in part as a result of a series of Westerns starring John Wayne. *(Peter Aleshire)*

Rainbow Bridge on the shores of Lake Powell at the southern edge of the Great Basin Desert was formed when the meander of a stream cut into a sandstone cliff. Erosion eventually cut all the way through the cliff, leaving behind an arch. Navajo creation myths have made the arch sacred to the Navajo. The once-remote arch can now be reached by boat on Lake Powell. *(Peter Aleshire)*

The Chihuahuan Desert and the Great Basin Desert are both considered cold deserts, which means they get some snow and many days of frost. As a result, the signature plants of the Sonoran Desert, like the frost-sensitive saguaro, cannot survive here. The cold-tolerant yucca and sagebrush take over. *(Peter Aleshire)*

The Chihuahuan Desert sprawls across northern Mexico and into the United States to places such as Organ Pipe National Monument where it gets enough rain to sustain a great diversity of large cacti, which survive the long months without water by storing moisture in their fleshy tissue. The monument forms a transition zone between the Chihuahuan and Sonoran Deserts, with a mixture of distinctive plants from both zones. *(Peter Aleshire)*

Barrel cactus like this one in full bloom cope with harsh desert conditions by storing large quantities of moisture in their tissues, pleated so that the cactus can expand significantly after a substantial but infrequent rainstorm. The bristling thorns, really modified leaves, both protect the moist tissues and provide shade from the sun that can heat the ground to more than 120° in the summer. *(Peter Aleshire)*

The Dragoon Mountains rise from the brushy expanses of a high, often cold, desert in southern Arizona. The Dragoons are part of a chain of north-south–running mountain ranges that create sky islands, relatively rich habitats surrounded by desert. This proved essential in sustaining Geronimo and other Apache raiders, who moved through these mountain ranges in and out of Mexico. *(Peter Aleshire)*

The San Pedro River in Arizona marks a blurry boundary between the Sonoran and Chihuahuan Deserts. One of the few reliable, undimmed rivers in all of the American Southwest, the San Pedro sustains a ribbon of cottonwoods and willows and offers a vital migratory highway for many of North America's migratory birds, which make their way up out of the Tropics and into Arizona before fanning out over North America. *(Peter Aleshire)*

Vanished rivers and seas deposited the sand that now forms great chains of dunes in Southwest Africa's Namib Desert. This star dune is nearly 300 feet (91.4 m) high. *(E. T. Nichols, U.S. Geological Survey)*

Sand slumps down the steep surface of this dune in Southwest Africa's Namib Desert, maintaining the striking geometry of a giant dune. *(E. D. McKee, U.S. Geological Survey)*

A wet winter and a mild spring produce one of the great incongruities of nature, brilliant wildflowers sprouting unexpectedly from the rocky soil of the Sonoran Desert. *(Peter Aleshire)*

Sand dunes and plants interact in complex ways, with plants serving to anchor dunes in place—providing they can grow fast enough to avoid burial. This curving linear dune ridge in the Simpson Desert of Australia exists in dynamic balance with the plants along its front face. *(E. D. McKee, U.S. Geological Survey)*

Salt deposits left by dried-up ice age lakes make bright white patches in the sea of sand in the Simpson Desert near Oodnadatta. *(E. D. McKee, U.S. Geological Survey)*

150-mile-long (241 km), 9,700-foot-tall (3 km), ecologically extravagant range of tormented rock is the most extensive and varied of southeast Arizona's famed Sky Islands and serves as a vivid lesson in how geology shapes both human and biological history.

Surrounded by desert grasslands and tenuously connected to the Chihuahuan Desert that lies mostly to the south and east, the darkly jagged crag of lava, ash, and limestone offers a refuge for a profusion of plants and animals, many of them throwbacks to the Ice Age now stranded on an igneous ark. The mountain's north-south alignment running down nearly to the Mexican border has shaped the history of the Arizona borderlands, providing a migratory corridor for elegant trogans, ghostly jaguars, doomed mammoths, desperate Apache, footsore soldiers, sweating settlers, saddle-sore rustlers, and lurking outlaws.

No other place in the Southwest has such a concentration of history and biology, all thanks to the jostling of continents, a titanic series of volcanic explosions, the churning of the atmosphere, and the accident of an international border.

The quirks of geography largely account for the violent and vivid characters that have wandered through its rugged canyons, rested alongside its gushing streams, and marveled at its eerie rock formations. Here the Apache chief Cochise waged his fierce and futile war, Geronimo extracted his insatiable revenge, Ike Clanton bought his stolen cattle, Johnny Ringo died in the arms of an oak tree, Wyatt Earp hunted his brothers' killers, Black Bart Ketchem fled with the loot from the stage, anthropologist-rancher Alden Hayes gathered folklore and pottery shards, and legions of oddballs, lunatics, and hard cases pitted themselves against the mountain and each other.

The Chiricahua National Monument's fused-ash spires, volcanic castles, balanced rocks, shaded streams and deep canyons offer the most scenic and best-exposed glimpse of the mountain's geology and ecology. The range also provided the setting for some of the most dramatic events in Western history, including the murder or suicide of outlaw Johnny Ringo, Wyatt Earp's bloody revenge for the death of his brothers, the adobe ruins of Fort Bowie where a young lieutenant provoked a decade-long war with Cochise, and a host of battlefields in that terrible war. Moreover, because of its remarkable geology, the range also harbors 83 mammal, 368 bird, and 75 reptile and amphibian species.

The story of today's landscape starts 27 million years ago when shifts deep in the Earth triggered millions of years of upheaval. These deep-seated geological forces cracked the crust, pushed up lines of mountains, and then stretched out the long, sunken basins separating those high ranges, isolating the Chiricahuas with low, wide valleys to the east and west. Meanwhile, molten rock accumulated miles beneath the surface, rising along fault lines and fractures until it hit the groundwater and carbon dioxide stored in buried layers of sediment, which prompted the magma to expand in volume 50-fold and created an unimaginable explosion of steam, lava, and ash. Massive clouds of superheated ash and pumice blasted out of a gigantic crater, down which broils of semiliquid rock hurled at 100 miles (161 km) an hour. The eruption ejected 100 cubic miles (416.8 cubic km) of debris, darkened the planet with its ash cloud, and covered 1,200 square miles (3,108 sq km). This volcanic ash flow eventually cooled and fused, creating the raw material for the spectacular rock formations of the Chiricahuas. The now-emptied *magma* crater collapsed, forming a 12-mile-wide (19 km), 5,000-foot-deep (1,524 m) crater.

Smaller eruptions continued for another 15 million years before the Earth's fury subsided and the eons of wind, ice, and erosion went to work to create the current landscape. Erosion filled in the giant crater, leaving only traces of its walls. Weathering and chemical deterioration sculpted the stone spires of the National Monument while fractures, erosion, and frost created the soaring monoliths of Cave Creek Canyon.

That long-ago volcanic outpouring shaped all subsequent history in the Chiricahuas. The Chiricahuas remain one of the most varied ecosystems in North America because of the overlap of four different zones, the Rocky Mountain, the Sierra Madre, the Sonoran Desert, and the Chihuahuan Desert. As a result, the mountains represent the northern limit for many tropical species, the southern limit for many North American species, and a migratory corridor for hundreds of others, including one of the most diverse collections of birds in the nation. The mountains serve as a northern equivalent of a rain forest.

During the last Ice Age, which ended about 10,000 years ago, abundant streams and an oak-juniper woodland connected the Chiricahuas with other mountain ranges. But as the climate dried out and a newly evolved desert scrub and grassland isolated the mountain, many species retreated to the wet upper elevations, nurtured by the establishment of summer monsoon patterns that deliver more than half of the annual 15 inches (381 mm) of rainfall during the normally heat-stressed summer months. As a result, the diversity of plants and animals here is astonishing, especially at the intersections of two of the world's great deserts.

For instance, the Chiricahuas boast just about the greatest diversity of hummingbird species in North America, plus 20 percent of the ant species found in the United States and Canada. The range also harbors hundreds of species of bees and four species of horny toads, bizarre, spiked flat-bodied throwbacks to cheesy dinosaur flicks, whose prominent spikes make them a potentially fatal snack for snakes. Each lizard consumes a couple hundred ants a day with their long, sticky tongues. Two of the horny toad species in the Chiricahuas are based in the harsh and arid Chihuahuan desert, one crawled up out of the wetter Sonoran desert, and one normally hangs out on mountaintops in Canada. They somehow divide up the terrain of the Chiricahuas thanks to fascinating adaptations. For instance, they stand in the rain and drink rainwater channeled to the corners of their mouths by the scales on their backs. They can also squirt blood out of their eye sockets that is especially irritating to coyotes, foxes, and unwary dogs.

This biological diversity explains why Cochise and Geronimo and a host of Apache warriors fought so desperately to hold onto the Chiricahuas during the Apache Wars that started when the Spanish ventured into the area in the 1500s and continued until Geronimo's surrender within sight of their pine-crowded peaks in 1886. The biological diversity of the mountains provided the Apache food in any season, crucial to the survival of a hunter-gatherer culture.

Cochise's Chiricahua Apache claimed the range when the Americans first arrived in the early 1800s and tried to maintain peace with the Americans when they wrested the region from Mexico in 1848. But a foolish army lieutenant trying to recover a rancher's son kidnapped by another band provoked a war with the formidable Cochise. His band killed hundreds of people in the course of the 1860s, until the government finally offered him a reservation that included the Chiricahuas and the nearby Dragoon Mountains farther west in the Sonoran Desert. However, soon after Cochise died the government shut down the reservation on the pretext of continued raids into Mexico. Most of the Chiricahua Apache sorrowfully marched off to the malarial flats of the San Carlos Reservation to the north. But others resumed the war, including Geronimo, resulting in another decade of bloody warfare that claimed hundreds of lives.

The mountains remain speckled with unmarked battlefields, especially in the infamous Apache Pass, with its stage line, Fort Apache, and the only reliable water for horses within 40 miles (64.4 km). Cochise, who once said that the rocks of the Chiricahuas and the Dragoons (shown in the color insert on page C-5) were his only friends, fought stubbornly for the mountains his people held sacred, but the Apache leaders who came after him could not hold onto them. A vivid new cast of characters moved into the mountain range once the army finally broke the stubborn resistance of the Apache and loaded them into cattle cars for what proved to be a devastating 28-year exile from the Southwest to a succession of disease-ridden prison camps.

Alden Hayes, who described himself as a "failed farmer, bankrupt cattleman, sometime smoke-chaser, one-time park ranger, and would-be *archaeologist*," spent decades gathering the remarkable stories of local ranchers who had hung on for generations, which he distilled into the wonderful *A Portal to Paradise*. He offered up the local versions of vivid Western history, including the feud between the Earps and the Clantons that produced the gunfight at the OK Corral, the Indian massacres, the strange death of gunfighter Johnny Ringo from a shot through the temple as he reclined bootless against a giant oak that still towers over Turkey Creek, the violent but inept career of Black Bart Ketcham who turned out to be two outlaws with the same name, and the remarkable life stories of hard cases like rancher-preacher-vigilante-pioneer-sometime-killer John Augustus Chenowth who first passed through the mountains in 1854, only to return in 1881 to make a life there. Chenowth led a massacre of probably peaceful Indians, faced down outlaws, killed his too-critical opponent for sheriff in a controversial case of "self-defense," said sermons over the people he killed, and founded a family dynasty that persists today in the wide, hard spaces of the Chiricahuas.

All of that biology, history, and geology remains mingled extravagantly on the steep, forested, fused-ash slopes of the Chiricahuas where hummingbirds zoom past the sites of forgotten massacres; butterflies flutter above lonely cemeteries crowded with crosses for the "unknown Mexican"; elegant trogans draw birders from distant continents to clump down dirt roads where Wyatt Earp hunted Johnny Ringo; and day hikers pause to marvel at the rock formations where 130 years ago the warriors of Cochise waited for the signal to begin shooting.

And above it all, the mountains loom like a monsoon thunderhead, grim and joyful, brimming with life and utterly without pity.

SAN PEDRO RIVER: A LINEAR OASIS

The San Pedro River marks the western edge of the Chihuahuan Desert. It is a small, struggling, vital, and enormously diverse river, thronged with ghosts. The last undammed river in a region where an estimated 90 percent of the precious riparian areas have been destroyed or degraded, the San Pedro nurtures great, leafy meanders of cottonwoods and willows. It is not endangered like so many already ruined desert rivers by groundwater pumping and drought, and it has sustained human beings for millennia. It remains one of the most diverse and vital places in this surprisingly rich desert country.

The San Pedro (shown in the color insert on page C-6) forms a linear oasis in the midst of an otherwise harsh desert, offering a respite for desert dwellers and a food-rich, ecological highway for other species that migrate from the winter-friendly tropics to the summer-bountiful sprawl of North America. That is why cottonwood and wetland habitats like the San Pedro rank as among the most biologically productive in the world and why more than 200 species of birds flutter through the multistoried canopy. It has also played a vital role in the history of the region as its water nourished ice age mammoth hunters, Spanish conquistadors, Apache raiders, pueblo builders, feuding gunfighters, desperate ranchers, bereaved fathers, arrogant mining magnates, and a host of other heroes and villains.

The human saga of the San Pedro starts for certain between 11,200 and 8,000 years ago, with the arrival of a mysterious group of big game hunters who tipped their sturdy stone spears with distinctively fashioned stone points, called Clovis points, named after where they were first discovered in Clovis, New Mexico. These Clovis culture hunters probably were descendants of people from Europe who crossed the Bering Strait between 50,000 and 15,000 years ago when the ice age expansion of the polar ice cap drew down the sea level and exposed the land bridge. The wandering hunter-gatherers fanned out across North America during the wet extravagance of the last ice age, undoubtedly following great herds of mammoths, camels, horses, bison, and tapirs. Paleontologists have identified some 37 important sites along the San Pedro where they have unearthed the bones of animals up to 7 million years old. They've also found at least two places where a combination of extinct animal bones and distinctive Clovis stone points denote an area where these big game hunters killed and butchered their prey. These finds make the San Pedro one of the best places in the country for studying the first appearance of human beings in North America and perhaps their impact on the awesome herds of gigantic animals like mammoths who became extinct in the face of human hunting and the climate change at the end of the Ice Age.

The San Pedro also harbors more than a dozen places where archaeologists have unearthed the remains of people of the Cochise culture, who occupied the area between 8,000 and 2,000 years ago. They probably discovered agriculture, but relied mostly on gathering wild plants and hunting the small game animals left after the disappearance of monsters like the mammoths and the sloths. They hunted with spears and chipped stone knives, made simple baskets, dry farmed almost wild corn crops, built simple brush shelters, and left behind a scattering of grinding stones and other tools. They also left behind scattered clues to a momentous discovery, the development of agriculture.

They were succeeded by outriders of the Mogollon, Hohokam, and Salado cultures between A.D. 1 and A.D. 1450. These people built pit houses and pueblos, dug irrigation ditches, planted corn, beans, and squash, fired pottery of beautiful shapes and designs, and incorporated the San Pedro River valley into a linked network of cultures that reached from California into New Mexico and down to the thriving empires of South America. This complex web of civilization collapsed in the 1400s for reasons that remain mysterious, but the San Pedro remained one of the few areas still occupied after the regional collapse.

The first Spanish explorers found the rich river valley occupied by the Sobaipuri Indians, who lived in small villages, built simple shelters, farmed the river bottom and terraces, and defended themselves from sporadic raiding by the warlike Apache Indians, recently arrived wanderers. Fray Marcos de Niza marched through the valley in 1539 and found the Sobaipuri friendly and anxious for an ally against their enemies, the Apaches. Francisco de Coronado's gigantic expedition in fruitless search for the mythical Seven Cities of Gold passed through the valley in the next year, and Father Eusebio Francisco Kino visited the Sobaipuri in 1692. Kino provided the Indians with seeds and cattle, but wasn't much help in fending off the Apaches. Ironically, the arrival of the Spanish may have actually escalated the Sobaipuri's war with the Apaches. The warrior culture of the Apaches quickly adapted to the horses and weapons of the Spanish and found that the horse and livestock herds the Spanish established around their missions greatly increased the payoff for conducting raids, which could now easily range over 1,000 miles (1,609 km) with the help of stolen horses.

Warfare with the Apaches escalated sharply with the arrival of the Spanish. In 1772 the Spanish decided to take advantage of the cooperative Sobaipuri on the San Pedro to help build the northernmost fort of their New World empire. They began construction of the Presidio de Santa Cruz de Terrenate in about 1776, dispatching several hundred soldiers and colonists to build an Apache-proof fortress. The Apaches quickly saw the danger and learned the fort's weak point. Built on an easily defensible bluff overlooking the river, the fort had no water or arable ground. The Spanish quickly discovered that working their fields or getting water could prove fatal. The harassing Apaches on one occasion even stole cattle and staged a rowdy feast on the riverbank in full view of the frustrated Spaniards, who never managed to get the walls built higher than four feet. Reluctantly, the Spanish abandoned the fort in 1780, having lost 80 men in their long war of attrition with the Apaches. Acknowledging defeat, the Spanish friars moved the Sobaipuri to a more defensible settlement near Tucson. This movement of the Sobaipuri out of the valley they had farmed for nearly 300 years suggests that the intervention of the Spanish had only served to increase the reach and appetite of the warrior Apaches.

The Apaches had the almost unrestricted run of the valley for nearly a century after the Spanish abandoned their presidio. No one dared settle the San Pedro Valley for decades after the soldiers left since the Apaches moved freely along the river corridor and remained secure from any reprisals in the surrounding mountains. In an effort to encourage settlement, however, the Mexican government in 1827 and 1833 made land grants to a great ranching family. They too eventually gave up in the face of continued Apache raiding. The Apaches, the Mexicans, and the arriving stream of American settlers waged a long, bitter struggle for control of the valley. The tide finally turned against the Apache in 1846 when the United States declared war on Mexico and claimed as spoils most of New Mexico, Arizona, and California.

The U.S. Army moved into and through the valley after the Mexican-American War ended in 1848. Clashes with the Apaches who still moved through the valley with relative impunity mounted steadily, coming to a head in the 1870s and 1880s.

The ultimate fate of the San Pedro River remained in the hands of a few large-scale ranchers, including George Hearst, the father of newspaper tycoon William Randolph Hearst. The ruthless, determined George Hearst built a vast, western empire. At one time, he owned some 7 million acres in the Mexican state of Chihuahua. He also served as a U.S. senator from California in the heyday of the robber barons when fabulously wealthy industrialists easily mingled economic and political power. George Hearst left most of his San Pedro valley ranch to his son and widow.

Another large chunk of the river was owned by Colonel William Greene, a mining millionaire. He was embroiled in several violent incidents, including a murder. Greene had built a dam along the San Pedro, but it burst, causing a flood that killed Greene's daughter. Greene suspected a rival, James Burnett, of sabotaging it. He grabbed his gun, found Burnett in a saloon, and shot him dead. Greene was tried and acquitted of murder charges.

Meanwhile, uncontrolled cattle grazing in the late 1880s spawned ecological disaster when drought struck in the 1890s. Overgrazing and

THE BATTLE OF THE BULLS

One of the strangest battles of the Mexican-American War was fought on the banks of the San Pedro. Under the leadership of Brigham Young, members of the Church of Latter-day Saints had settled in Mexico seeking a refuge from religious persecution when the Mexican-American War broke out. Young believed that if he offered the United States a company of men to help fight Mexico, he could win tolerance, transportation, and desperately needed cash. So after threatening to enlist women, children, and old people if fighting-age men didn't volunteer, Brigham Young mustered 500 volunteers, who lined up raggedly under the command of Phillip St. George Cooke and set out to develop a road between the Rio Grande and California. Like Coronado before them, they passed through the San Pedro River valley.

On the banks of the San Pedro they fought their only battle when a herd of enraged, wild bulls attacked the wagon train. The astonished soldiers found themselves beset by scores of furious bulls, which seemed to be more enraged than hurt by bullets. The bulls, descended from cattle abandoned by the Mexicans and the Spanish, badly gored two men and killed several mules. The well-armed Mormons ultimately killed about 20 bulls and probably wounded about twice that many.

extermination of beavers worked dramatic ecological changes. Once the San Pedro was a long marsh created by beaver dams, fringed by an extensive mesquite forest. Thick grass covered the uplands, protecting the powdery soil. The marshes soaked up floods, and cottonwoods and willows provided a rich wildlife habitat. The overgrazing and the drought first killed millions of cattle, then resulted in the drying out of much of the river. In the process, the nature of the surrounding grassland was permanently altered, as grasses gave way to mesquite scrub and the land shifted toward desert.

A coalition of conservationist groups spearheaded by the Sierra Club and the Nature Conservancy eventually convinced the federal government to save the San Pedro through land swaps that created a 56,000-acre conservation area along 17 miles of the river's course. The federal government has since kept out cattle and brought back beaver, which has begun to restore the cottonwoods, grasses, and marshes that make the river so biologically rich. Sadly, a recent decade-long drought coupled with groundwater pumping in nearby towns have reduced flows and once again the river is threatened.

Section II

Deradse
around the World

✧✧✧✦✧✧✧

5

Sahara Desert

Northern Africa

Something happened. Something bad. Something strange. Some 6,000 years ago, the region of North Africa that today constitutes the world's greatest desert was a lush grassland studded with scrubby trees, lakes, and streams. Antelope, rhinos, hippos, lions, jackals, giraffes, clams, fish, and human beings wandered about in well-*hydrated* content. That hospitable grassland habitat dated back at least 400,000 years, according to various studies.

The implications are enormous. Today the Sahara Desert covers almost all of Northern Africa—about 3.3 million square miles (8.6 million sq km). Some areas of this 3,000-mile-wide (4,800 km) swath of rocky desolation and stunning sand dunes form a terrible barrier that cuts off most of the creatures living in Africa from Europe. Between 400,000 and 100,000 years ago, when the first humans were spreading out of southern Africa to populate the planet, they could easily pass through the welcoming grasslands of the Sahara, hunting the same big game animals they evolved alongside in southern Africa.

This grassland affected the course of human history by providing an ecological highway that enabled human beings to spread out of Africa to every other continent. And today, ongoing changes on the margins of the planet's harshest desert have provided clues to current changes in the Earth's climate. Moreover, the abrupt transformation of this grassland into desert between 4,000 and 6,000 years ago may have helped spur the development of western civilization.

Researchers have found the answers to vital questions as they have studied the massive sand dunes, dried lake beds, and scattered stone tools in a desert that is 1,200 miles (1,900 km) deep and 3,000 miles (4,800 km) wide with bizarre wildlife, singing dunes, and ancient secrets.

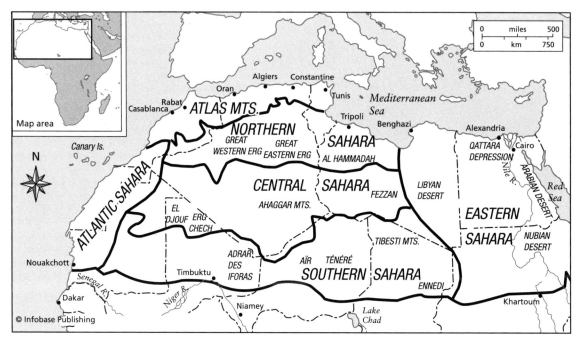

Sahara Desert

CAN SNAIL SHELLS SOLVE A MYSTERY?

Things have changed dramatically in the Sahara, according to Washington University Assistant Professor of Earth Sciences Jennifer Smith, who has studied ancient snail shells taken from some of the Sahara's vanished lakes. Specifically, she dug shells of the freshwater gastropod *Melanoides* out of silts laid down in the bottom of a small lake in the Kharga oasis of western Egypt. She concluded that 130,000 years ago tool-using human beings lived along the shores of the lake, along with hippos, giraffes, and other wildlife.

As it happens, this was the very period when the genetic and archaeological evidence suggests human beings were migrating through this lake-graced savannah and then fanning out across Europe, Asia, and North America. DNA analysis has already shown that all modern human beings alive today have a common ancestor who lived in southern Africa between 70,000 and 180,000 years ago. Although other upright walking hominids lived on other continents, they all apparently vanished as modern *homo sapiens* spread out across the planet. Therefore, the state of the Sahara grassland 130,000 years ago has a direct bearing on all of human evolution.

The Washington University researchers dug through 15-foot-thick (5 m) silt layers on the now dry lake bed, most of it laid down during a wet phase that lasted for thousands of years. Today, the area gets only a trace of rain. But 130,000 years ago, the rainfall averaged 23 inches (600 mm) per year. The researchers analyzed the shells of 20 freshwater snails, because the chemical composition of the shells gives a clue to past climate. The snails incorporate into their hard shells certain *isotopes* that indicate whether the lake in which they were living was stable or subject to strong evaporation. Lakes that are evaporating have higher concentrations of salt and other minerals in the water, like today's Salton Sea or Dead Sea. The researchers measured the calcium carbonate levels in the silts of the long-vanished lake and the isotopes the snails had incorporated into their shells. The scientists paid special attention to elements sensitive to evaporation rates. The study demonstrated that 130,000 years ago the lake had a stable water level with only modest net evaporation for long periods of time.

A MYSTERY 1,000 YEARS OLDER THAN STONEHENGE

Other studies have shown that human beings thrived in the Sahara for 100,000 years or more in areas now virtually uninhabitable. For instance, scientists have discovered the earliest known observatory for marking the movement of the stars, which ancient people could have used in religious ceremonies and in planning their migrations and crop plantings. Some 6,500 years ago at Nabta in Egypt, ancient people somehow positioned in a circle a series of flat, tomblike stone structures to which they connected five lines of now-toppled stone monoliths. These vanished Sahara dwellers positioned their heavy stone monuments a full 1,000 years before the mysterious builders of Stonehenge in England. The ruins lie on the shoreline of an ancient lake that filled some 11,000 years ago, but dried up an estimated 4,800 years ago. Beneath one of the stone structures researchers found a rock carved into the shape of a cow standing upright. They also found several ritually buried cows, laid reverently to rest in a roofed, clay-lined chamber. The stone circle measures 12 feet (4 m) in diameter, with alignments that apparently mark the position of the sun on *summer solstice*, the longest day of the year. The alignment of the stones also point to two stone megaliths about a mile away, although scientists still do not fully understand the significance of some of the alignments. The ancient observatory was right on the shore of the lake and may have been designed to mark the high-water mark of the lake's seasonal expansion. The researchers noted that it now appears that the desert-dwellers who arranged the stone monoliths at Nabta may have moved to the banks of the Nile River as the Sahara dried, perhaps in their movement fostering the emergence of the Egyptian civilization, one of the first, irrigation-based civilizations in human history.

TELLTALE STONE TOOLS YIELD CLUES

Other studies have yielded similar conclusions and demonstrated how important the much-wetter Sahara was to human beings as they developed the culture and technology that would eventually enable them to dominate ecosystems on every continent. For instance, mysterious nomads wandered across the Sahara Desert between 8,000 and 5,500 years ago, according to a National Science Foundation study conducted by Angela Close, a University of Washington anthropologist.

These Stone Age people apparently used cattle to move sandstone boulders from which they manufactured the stone tools they used to harvest the wild grasses that then grew in certain areas of the Sahara. Already, the stable, moist conditions that had sustained the freshwater snails had waned, but summer monsoons still brought the rainfall totals to about 8 inches (203 mm) a year—about the same as the present-day Sonoran Desert in North America, perhaps the lushest of all modern deserts (shown in the color insert on page C-7). Because the Sahara dried out during this time, the stone tools of these vanished hunters and gatherers remain scattered near the surface rather than buried or carried off by rain as they would have been anyplace else. Moreover, few people have ventured into the forbidding wasteland of the Sahara in the past 5,000 years, which means these clues to the past remain undiscovered on the surface.

Close found that the area around the Bir Safsaf oasis some 570 miles (900 km) southwest of Cairo was dominated by a series of great, sand-covered ripples extending for 100 to 500 yards and rising three to six feet (1–3 m) above the sandy plain. Between the ripples, the monsoon rains of that wetter desert collected. This nourished a summer crop of grasses in the depressions between these natural features. That combination of water and grass drew the nomads between 5,000 and 8,000 years ago as they struggled to make a living in the gradually drying desert.

Close realized that the scattering of stone tools might tell her a lot about the people who once lived there. She could tell that some were made of sandstone hardened by a dash of quartz, which had to come from outcroppings some 10 to 13 miles (16–21 km) away. Clearly, they had gone to great effort in hauling boulders of tool-making sandstone great distances to these ripples and depressions so they could chip off stone tools to harvest the grasses. She also found some tools made of flint, which had to have come from outcroppings 90 miles (145 km) away.

Close gathered up every single fragment of a stone tool plus every chip flaked off the larger boulders when making such tools within five square miles. She then fit those pieces of stone together like a giant jigsaw puzzle. She eventually collected 5,000 artifacts, which she spent years matching up with one another and with the boulders from which they had been chipped.

She concluded first that they had used cattle to haul their precious boulders. Moreover, the pattern of the tool scatter demonstrated that they spent their lives moving from one ripple to another, setting up camp alongside the low, water-catching spaces between the ripples and using their stone tools to harvest the grass. In effect, they were early wheat farmers.

So the research shows a slow drying of the Sahara between 130,000 years ago and 6,000 years ago. However, some time between 4,000 and 6,000 years ago, the transition to today's harsh desert escalated dramatically.

A DEVASTATING DESERT EXPANSION

Starting around 6,000 years ago, the Sahara Desert started an abrupt and devastating expansion. In a geological blink of an eye, the boundary between hard-core desert and grassland shifted by about 500 miles (800 km), which increased the size of the desert by nearly 50 percent. Moreover, the summer monsoons that had sustained the grass-harvesters with the quartz-sandstone tools failed. Areas of the desert that used to get 8–10 inches (200–254 mm) of rain in a year dried out so that they received only 3–4 inches (76–101 mm). Reliable rainfall in several different seasons gave way to a new climate in which sometimes no rain fell at all for years at a time in some areas. Suddenly, grasslands that once harbored elephants, giraffes, and other large animals could shelter only camels. Areas that once blossomed after summer rains withered and subsided into sandy desert silence.

Climate researchers have worked hard to understand the abrupt change, especially since the Sahara Desert has been expanding again in recent decades. Several studies suggest that the change some 6,000 years ago was caused by a small shift in the Earth's orbit and axis of rotation, compounded by a feedback effect caused by the response of plants and dust storms.

The root cause was connected to a change in the amount of solar radiation reaching Earth. The Earth's orbit around the sun varies slightly from year to year. As a result, during certain periods the Earth does not get quite as close to the sun at the near point of its annual orbit. The timing of that close approach also shifts, causing a realignment of the seasons. Moreover, the Earth wobbles just slightly as it spins on its axis, like a top.

Some 9,000 years ago, Earth's tilt was 24.14 degrees, compared to the current 23.45 degrees. In addition, the Earth's closest approach to the sun came some six months sooner than it does now. These small changes in Earth's spin and orbit gradually destabilized the planet's climate. For instance, the shift in seasons resulted in the Northern Hemisphere receiving more summer sunlight, which increased the power of the African and Indian summer monsoons. That shift in the timing and strength of the monsoons in turn dramatically affected rainfall patterns in the Sahara.

Ironically, the abrupt expansion of the Sahara Desert may have played a key role in spurring the rise of Western civilization. The great irrigation-based civilizations of the Middle East that arose along the Nile, Tigris, and Euphrates rivers all coincided with this period of climate change and desert expansion. Perhaps the climate shift forced the nomadic desert dwellers that had lived for tens of thousands of years off the bounty of the grasslands and the summer monsoons into the fertile river valleys. That concentration of population and the need to develop irrigation systems to compensate for the fickle rainfall may have given rise to the increasingly complex civilizations of the Middle East. The descendents of Sahara grasslands dwellers living along these river valleys went on to build the pyramids, invent writing, and lay the groundwork for many of the world's religions.

BLAME THE PLANTS FOR SPEED OF SAHARA EXPANSION

It is important to note that even after taking into account the effects of the Earth's wobble and the shift in summer temperatures, climate experts cannot account for the speed with which the grasses withered and the Sahara expanded.

Blame the plants, concluded a team of German scientists led by Martin Claussen, which published its results recently in *Geophysical Research Letters*. The researchers concluded that the atmosphere, oceans, clouds, and plants all respond to changes in climate in ways that can greatly magnify the effects. The scientists used a supercomputer to calculate those effects. For instance, as grassland turns to desert the plants work many changes. Plants hold water, stabilize soils, absorb solar energy, take in carbon dioxide, release oxygen, increase humidity, and affect how much water goes into streams. They also hold down topsoil, which has a big impact on how much dust rises in great billows from the surface of the desert. That dust, in turn, affects rainfall patterns. So as the climate heats, the plants falter, which makes the land more prone to *erosion* during the increasingly infrequent heavy rains. The increased erosion and lack of plant cover stir up more dust, which can further decrease rainfall.

Some scientists who studied the startling expansion of the Sahara to roughly its present size some 6,000 years ago concluded that the changes were abrupt, taking place in a span of decades rather than centuries. So clearly, the evolution of the Sahara Desert represents a disturbing, cautionary tale for scientists and policy makers worried about the current effects of global warming caused by the release of pollutants and deforestation.

THE GEOLOGY OF THE SAHARA

Today, the vast, hostile Sahara remains the mother of all deserts. High points like 11,204-foot (3,415 m) Mount Koussi in Chad rise like stone fortresses in a great battlefield of sand. A series of ridges and mountain ranges are separated by great, stretched, low-lying depressions, like the Quyattara Depression of Egypt that lies 436 feet (143 m) below sea level.

Named for the Arabic word for desert, *sahra*, this vast region sits on top of the warped, deformed, and folded African Shield, composed of some of the oldest rocks on the planet, forged when life was limited to single-celled creatures living in the oceans. These older rocks underlying the present-day Sahara are mostly granite, schist, or *gneiss*, all mixtures of igneous and metamorphic rocks forged deep beneath the surface. The rocks that form the African Shield were laid down near the surface, buried, remelted, re-fused, and returned finally to the surface. The African Shield comprises the hard bedrock of Africa and has held the continent together during the hundreds of millions of years that it has been split, shifted, twisted, and rammed into Europe as a result of the movement of the crustal plates.

This stable mass of rock has been covered over with younger sediments, laid down in horizontal, largely unaltered layers. Much of the Sahara is covered with limestone, made mostly of the skeletons of microscopic sea creatures raining down onto the bottom of a vanished sea. Most of the limestone and sandstone covering the surface of the Sahara were deposited in the *Mesozoic* era (245–65 million years ago). This was the heyday of the dinosaurs, encompassing their rise in the Triassic period and their mysterious extinction at the end of the Cretaceous period. In the Mesozoic era, both mammals and birds emerged to spread over the surface of the Earth when the dinosaurs faltered. Moreover, at the same time, the evolution of plants transformed life on land. Strange ferns, *cycads*, ginkgophytes, and other types dominated the surface at the beginning of the period. But by the end, flowering plants and conifers had largely displaced them.

The limestone and sandstone laid down when the dinosaurs were gobbling one another were established in vast lakes and seas when the hard underlying rock of the African Shield got heated and deeply buried in the restless jostling of continents. The basins caused by the stretching of the crust over the down-warping rocks of the shield filled with huge bodies of water like the ancient Mega-Chad. Many of these rocks now have that distinctive feature of the desert, a rich, reddish-brown coating of iron and manganese compounds weathered into desert varnish. The plateaus of the Sahara are covered with such dark, varnished rock.

Closer to the center of the great desert, several massive volcanic eruptions caused by the stresses and strains of these continental collisions left great, isolated mountain ranges or massifs. These include the highest points of the Sahara, the Tibesti and Ahaggar mountains, plus Mount Uwaynat.

THE WORLD'S BIGGEST SAND DUNES

The Sahara is best known for its massive sand dunes. These sand dunes cover about one-quarter of the Sahara, the tallest, most complex, most extensive dune fields in the world. These dunes are the result of powerful, constant, continental winds moving sand left over from a time when the Sahara had lakes, streams, and floods, all of which have left their silts and sands lying in the depressions with barely a root to hold them down. Some pyramid-shaped dunes in the Sahara tower 500 feet (167 m) tall. Some of the mountainous sand ridges that cross the desert reach heights of 1,000 feet (330 m), made almost entirely of fine-grained sand. As seen in the color insert on page C-7, those shifting fields of dunes dwarf similar features in other deserts, like the red dunes of Monument Valley in the Great Basin Desert or the smaller dune fields near Yuma in the Mojave Desert.

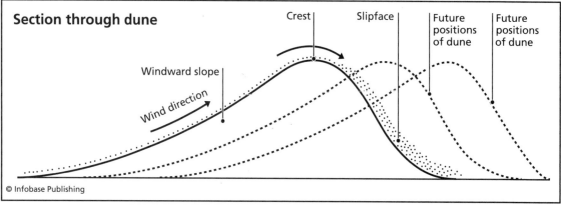

Sand dunes

Sand dunes mark the limits of many deserts, usually formed from sand first deposited along rivers or shallow seas. The presence of the dunes in most of the world's great deserts testify to a time when wetter conditions prevailed, creating the rivers that deposited the sand that now define the waterless deserts. *(Peter Aleshire)*

SAND DUNES SING

The dunes of the Sahara sometimes sing by emitting a low, haunting humming or booming sound. The still poorly explained sound puzzled some early explorers. Marco Polo in the 13th century blamed, "evil desert spirits [which] at times fill the air with the sounds of all kinds of musical instruments and also of drums and the clash of arms." Modern researchers have recorded low-pitched rumbles audible for 10 miles (16 km), sometimes coming daily from certain dunes. Some researchers think that the sounds are caused by some kind of vibration that is picked up and amplified by the quartz crystals.

University of Paris researcher Bruno Andreotti recorded the 95-hertz rumble coming from one dune in Morocco, one of 35 known singing dunes. The best singers appear to be large, crescent-shaped dunes. Such dunes can belt out sounds two or three times in an afternoon when the wind kicks up. Andreotti concluded that the sounds are emitted when wind knocks loose an avalanche of extra dry sand on a slope of at least 35 degrees. On the other hand, some smaller dunes only sing when it is hot and there is no wind, according to research in the *Physical Review of Letters*. Clearly, something about the slide of sand down the face of the dune causes the humming, which Andreotti and his team demonstrated by starting sand slides that triggered the sound. The hum started during a slow-motion sand slide. Apparently, the curve of the dune acts as a loudspeaker to broadcast the sound of the sliding sand. The ringing of the quartz crystals in the sand smacking against one another 100 times per second somehow sets up a feedback loop, like the ear-splitting screech from an amplified speaker. In the case of the dune, the sounds Andreotti recorded have the pitch of a low-flying propeller plane or a drum, broadcast at about the volume of a snowblower. Still, no one knows why so few dunes sing and what constitutes the critical difference between a singing dune and the great mute majority.

THE GHOST OF WATER

Most of the rugged, sandy terrain of the Sahara drains into expansive internal basins or, in the north, into the ghostly tributaries of the Nile River. A few rivers that arise beyond the limits of the desert drain into it, contributing to its fitful supply of streams and its ancient supply of groundwater.

The greatest inflow of water comes from the high, tropical areas to the south, most of which feed their waters into the Nile to flow north along the eastern edge of the Sahara and into the Mediterranean. Several empty into Lake Chad in the southern part of the desert and others empty into the internal basins. Very few flow year round. Mostly, the drainage system of the Sahara is dry and fitful, save on the margins of the great, interior desert space. The desert is embroidered with mostly dry washes called wadis, the fitfully active remnants of the system of rivers and streams that sustained the hunters and gatherers who cut grass with stone tools 6,000 years ago. Now, those wadis generally carry rain after the stray storm that struggles past the barrier of rising, heated desert air.

Sometimes, those dry watercourses carry substantial flash floods, since rooted plants do not hold back the runoff.

The Sahara's lack of topsoil as a result of the breakdown of the nutrients from the remains of plants in the upper layers of soil renders most of the desert barren. Few areas can yield decent crops even when wells provide water, mostly for the lack of nitrogen and organic remains that sustain plants. In some areas, bacteria ekes out a living on the few organic remains. That bacteria in the soil can produce the free nitrogen plants need to survive. But those barely fertile areas lie mostly along the wadis or atop underground reservoirs of water. The low-lying areas that might collect organic debris that could make for good topsoil often also have high concentrations of salts and minerals from the evaporation of water from the surface. As a result, even where soils might build up, salts sharply limit plant growth. Free carbonates in the upper levels of

LIVING ON MILLION-YEAR-OLD WATER

One recent study demonstrated that the Sahara's hidden but increasingly hard-pressed supply of groundwater is actually fossil water that fell as rain more than a million years ago. This source of groundwater fell from the sky when the African continent was farther south, the current Mediterranean Sea was a low-lying desert, and the Sahara was a wet grassland. The underground water has been flowing to the north for eons, according to a study by scientists at Argonne National Laboratory published in *Geophysical Research Letters*.

The Argonne researchers developed an ingenious way to determine the age of ancient water. When cosmic rays spit out by the sun hit molecules of water floating about in the air, the impact creates an unstable isotope of the faintly radioactive element *krypton*. A regular krypton atom hit by a cosmic ray may absorb the energy and become krypton 81. This isotope will eventually release the extra energy and revert to normal krypton, although the process takes an average of about 500,000 years. As rain falls through the atmosphere, it picks up these isotopes of krypton. Once the water soaks into the ground, the clock starts ticking on the conversion of krypton 81 into regular krypton. So if physicists can measure the ratio between regular krypton and krypton 81, they can estimate how long ago the water in the underground water table fell through the sky as raindrops. However, that requires finding a way to detect the almost impossibly rare atoms of krypton 81 in water samples taken from wells in the Sahara. In the atmosphere, only one out of 1 trillion krypton atoms are the rare krypton 81, and raindrops absorb only a tiny percentage of the free-floating krypton atoms on their plunge toward Earth. Fortunately, the scientists used the ultrasensitive Atom-Trap Trace Analysis to spot a few krypton 81 atoms in the groundwater.

The results showed that almost all of the water now in the underground aquifers in the Sahara fell as rain between 200,000 and 1 million years ago. That means that even when the Sahara was a grassland 130,000 years ago, very little rainwater soaked in deep enough to join the aquifers.

soil demonstrate that in its current desert state, very little water soaks into the soil to reach the hidden water table. Most of the water that does make it to the upper few inches of soil quickly evaporates back into the atmosphere, which is the defining hallmark of a desert.

IN THE GRIP OF A DRY CLIMATE

The Sahara remains the preeminent example of a midlatitude desert formed as a result of the way in which heating at the equator drives the atmospheric circulation of the whole planet. Moist, heated air rises high into the atmosphere at the equator, which draws the steady flow of the trade winds in the midlatitudes. The air from the equator drops most of its moisture as it rises and cools, which nourishes the tropical rain forests that girdle the equator. The now-dry air flows north in the Northern Hemisphere, cooling as it rises. Eventually, this cold, heavy, dry air sinks toward the surface to replace the air rushing toward the equator in the form of the steady trade winds. All around the globe, deserts mark where this dry air drops to the surface.

The Sahara started its intermittent desert phase some 5 million years ago, when the continents moved into more or less their present condition and planetary atmospheric circulation patterns took their present form. Ever since, the Sahara has gone through cycles of long-term climatic drought, sometimes lush grassland and sometimes harsh desert.

Human beings in the past 7,000 years may have actually helped extend or maintain those periods of greater moisture by growing crops and grazing cattle. The climate and extent of the desert has been especially stable in the past 2,000 years. However, shifts in the Earth's orbit and tilt plus the feedback effects of wind patterns and climate have resulted in a few unusual periods, like the Little Ice Age of the 16th through the 18th centuries.

Climatically, the Sahara breaks down into northern and southern halves. In the south, the dry subtropical climate features very high temperature ranges, freezing winters, scalding summers, and rainfall peaks in both summer and winter. This climate supports more plants, animals, and humans than the much harsher north. In the north, stable high-pressure cells centered over the tropic of Cancer ward off any rain-bearing clouds. In this area, the average annual daily temperature range is about 68°F (20°C), with hot summers and cold winters. The Sahara claims the hottest temperature ever recorded—136°F (48°C) in Libya on the northern edge of the Sahara. Rainfall averages a scant 3 inches (76 mm) per year. Most of the rain falls in the winter, but summer thunderstorms can produce major floods. Moreover, strong, steady *haboob* winds can swirl the

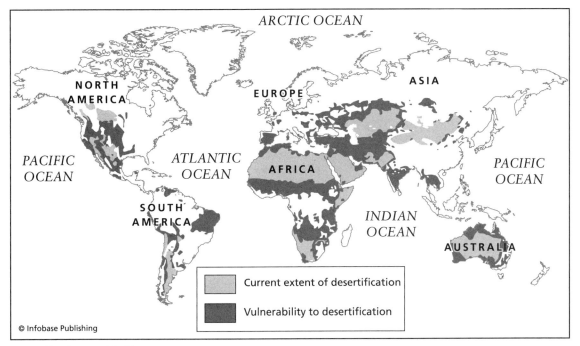

Desertification worldwide

dust of the Sahara into the mid- to upper atmosphere, so that it settles on the far side of the world.

PLANTS OUTWIT DROUGHT AND HEAT

Few plants can deal with the combination of heat, cold, and dehydration. Large areas in the shifting dune fields have only a handful of plants struggling to grow fast enough to avoid burial. In the low-lying areas that once held great lakes, only salt-tolerant halophytes can detoxify concentrations of salt and minerals that would cause the cells of normal plants to rupture. Any desert plant must have evolved ways to cope with the heat and dryness. Some put down deep, broad root systems. Some grow only in sheltered areas. Many germinate within days of a good rain and sprint through their life cycle in a race against heat and dehydration, living in a frenzy to scatter seeds that can await the next big rain. The scattered volcanic mountain ranges harbor survivors from earlier, wetter times, since the upper reaches of an 11,000-foot (3,352 m) mountain may have conditions today similar to the conditions that existed near the base of the mountain 10,000 years ago. Woody Sahara plants among these ice age survivors include species of the olive, cypress, and mastic trees.

When ancient, underground water comes to the surface in an oasis, other hardy desert survivors like doum palm, oleander, date palm, thyme, and acacia seek out a survivor's foothold. So do salt-tolerant plants like tamarisk, or salt cedar, which people brought from Africa to plant in the American Southwest to use as windbreaks a century ago. Since then, the salt cedar has spread throughout waterways in the American desert to become a major pest. Hardened in the Sahara Desert, the salt cedar has proved formidable competition along the degraded riparian areas of the American West.

ANIMALS ALSO EVOLVE INGENUOUS ADAPTATIONS

The Sahara once had a broad, vital array of animal species, including elephants, lions, ostrich, and a host of other species. But many animals vanished as the climate shifted, the desert expanded, and human beings killed off the fragile survivors. For instance, a hunter killed the last known antelopelike addax in the northern Sahara in the early 1920s, and other species are on the brink of extinction. Now, only a handful of animals live in the deep desert. Many of the unique species that thousands of years ago took refuge on the arklike volcanic islands rising from the sea of sand barely survive. Remaining desert animals include the gerbil, jerboa, Cape hare, desert hedgehog, anubis baboon, spotted hyena, jackal, sand fox, Libyan striped weasel, slender mongoose, Barbary sheep, scimitar-horned oryx, dorcas gazelle, dama deer, and Nubian wild ass. Some 300 birds have been spotted at some point in the Sahara, but most are passing through on migration routes that originate in the Tropics and fan out across Europe and Asia. Many of the birds move along the coastal areas without braving the interior. However, some birds do make use of the vast expanses of the interior desert, including ostriches, Nubian bustards, desert eagle owls, fan-tailed ravens, and a handful of others.

WHAT LIES AHEAD FOR THE SAHARA?

The Sahara remains the most sparsely inhabited place on the planet, with the exception of the frozen wastes of Antarctica. Most of the herders and traders who once made a living here have vanished, their cultures crushed by contact with outsiders and shifts in trade routes that no longer require goods to cross the harsh desert. Various mineral deposits and oil have spurred some economic activity, including iron, copper, *manganese*, uranium, phosphates, coal, oil, and natural gas. But most deposits are scattered, and the lack of water has prevented large-scale development of long-term settlements that sometimes outlive mining booms.

Mostly, those economic booms have left the desert even more harsh by using up the million-year-old water stored underground. The sharp drop in water table levels has been blamed for complex changes that have largely destroyed the ancient lifestyles of the desert people. For instance, the increasing aridity has increased the threat of locust plagues as the ravenous grasshopperlike insects have focused on the more concentrated green areas. As the dropping water tables dry up oases and rare springs, the people of the desert have grown increasingly concentrated, which has triggered other environmental changes.

As a result of those local changes and the warming of the planet in the past century, the Sahara has resumed its expansion after 2,000 years of relative stability. As a result, the Sahara may once again play a crucial role in shaping the climate of the whole planet because of its ability to generate massive dust storms.

Climate experts have measured a significant increase in average temperatures planetwide in the past century. Most climate scientists blame much of the increase on the significant increase in carbon dioxide in the atmosphere as a result of human pollution, including power plants and automobiles. Carbon dioxide does not block the long wavelengths of light entering the atmosphere from the sun, but it does absorb the shorter wavelength infrared radiation reflected by the sun-warmed rocks, soil, and plants on the surface. As a result, the increasing concentrations of carbon dioxide trap heat in the lower atmosphere, warming up the surface of the planet.

That has apparently caused an expansion of the desert and higher summer temperatures. That, in turn, pours extra energy into the wind currents that created the Sahara in the first place. The increasing wind has driven a significant increase in Sahara dust storms. Moreover, the windstorms themselves seem to decrease rainfall, which reduces plant life, increases temperatures, and therefore drives even more wind. This perfectly illustrates the way in which temperatures can create unexpected feedback loops that exaggerate the effect.

Increasing the dust in the air can reduce rainfall over a wide area, according to a recent NASA study published in *The Proceedings of the National Academy of Sciences*. The results surprised scientists, who thought that putting more dust particles into the air might increase rainfall by giving the water vapor in clouds particles to form around, which they thought would create more and bigger raindrops. In fact, the opposite seems to happen, according to a study that compared satellite measurements of clouds with rainfall measurements on the ground. Apparently when dust particles enter a cloud, very small water droplets form on the vastly increased number of particles. These abnormally small water droplets hit each other, break up, and then reform without growing large enough for gravity to overcome air resistance and make them fall out of the cloud. As a result, rain clouds seeded with dust particles hang onto their moisture much longer. Therefore, the clouds that drift over desert areas that generate big dust clouds more often move on without dropping their moisture. As a result, the dust created by the expansion of the desert drives away the rain, which in turn increases the rate of desertification. This tendency of dust to increase desertification could play a surprising and unexpected role in shaping the planet's climate in the face of global warming. Perhaps it even played a role in the rapid expansion of the Sahara Desert 6,000 years ago.

Already, the dust of the Sahara has been showing up in some unexpected places. Saharan dust blown up into the atmosphere has increased significantly in recent decades, for reasons scientists don't fully understand. Some studies show that dust kicked up into the atmosphere by storms in the Sahara can affect cloud formation across the north Atlantic, according to an analysis of satellite data. Other studies have shown that African dust blown out of the Sahara appears to trigger lethal outbreaks of meningitis, probably because the dust irritates people's nasal passages and that makes it easier for meningitis spores to enter their bloodstreams. Surprisingly, African dust makes up one-half of the breathable particles in the air over Miami, Florida. As a result, some drifting Saharan dust storms can actually trigger clean air alerts in Miami when they drift into town. In yet another surprising fallout from African dust, some doctors fear that the high iron content in African dust could cause more health and lung problems even in North America, according to a study published recently by the *American Geophysical Union.*

Already, this increase in wind, desertification, and dust storms could be affecting the climate, according to several alarming bits of evidence. *Glaciologist* Lonnie Thompson and a research team at Ohio State University have been comparing the air trapped in 6,000-year-old glaciers to today's atmosphere. This fossil air trapped in bubbles when the ice froze 6,000 years ago can reveal the composition of the atmosphere during the period stone tool–wielding nomads finally abandoned the Sahara as the desert expanded. Thompson combined the analysis of that fossil air with other clues, including tree-ring data from Ireland and England that provides a rainfall record going back 7,000 years. Those lines of evidence both suggested that the rapid expansion of the Sahara 6,000 years ago corresponded to a planetary drought. However, the speed of the changes did not quite match the scope of the changes noted in the past 100 years. Already, 10,000-year-old glaciers have been melting all over the planet, from the top of Africa's Mount Kilimanjaro to the high peaks of the Peruvian Andes.

Thompson's team concluded that the climate changed abruptly 5,200 years ago and the Sahara expanded by perhaps 50 percent in a matter of decades. He suggested that the speed of that change shows that although natural feedback loops may hold back climate change up to a point, those feedback loops also may greatly accelerate change once conditions go past a certain threshold. That is a worrisome finding in a time when carbon dioxide and temperature levels are rising measurably each year.

6

Arabian Desert

Middle East

The great, sand-swirled Arabian Desert that includes almost all of modern-day Iraq and Saudi Arabia is all about beginnings, both the genesis of Western civilization and the birth of an ocean. Moreover, the remarkable geology of the region sustains modern civilization with the compressed ooze of eons past in the form of the world's most extensive deposits of oil.

The 900,000-square-mile (2.33 million sq km) Arabian Desert is in many ways a continuation of the larger Sahara Desert that covers most of Northern Africa. The same global climate patterns that baked the Sahara also made the Arabian Peninsula a great desert—the hot, humid air that rises at the equator, drops its moisture on the rain forests, then descends as a dry scourge over both the Sahara and the Arabian Peninsula.

In the north, the Arabian Desert blends into the Negev Desert of Israel and the nearly deserted Sinai Peninsula. It encompasses all of the Arabian Peninsula bounded by the Red Sea on the west and the Persian Gulf on the east. It also includes the oil-rich nations of Kuwait, Bahrain, Oman, Yemen, and the United Arab Emirates.

This sweeping desert has played a vital role in human history. For instance, the whole area has only one significant river system, the Tigris-Euphrates and their tributaries. These rivers essentially gave rise to Western civilization. The rivers could sustain farming in the midst of a harsh desert, but only if people cooperated sufficiently to build the large-scale irrigation works needed to divert water on the fertile floodplains of the flood-prone desert rivers. This need for social cohesion and organization in the Fertile Crescent gave rise to the first complex Western civilizations, starting about 5,000 years ago. The same process took place along the Nile, another great desert river. By about 2500 B.C. the Assyrian civilization had organized a large area. The civilizations of this area developed the crops that fed subsequent civilizations, domesticated cattle and other animals, invented writing, and passed down a rich legacy, including the lock and key, the 60-minute hour, postal systems, flush toilets, aqueducts, magnifying glasses, and the arch. In a very real sense, the challenges of coping with a desert environment gave rise to modern civilization.

THE BIRTH OF AN OCEAN

Even today, the geology of this desert caught between Africa and Eurasia remains dynamic. For instance, the Earth's crust is splitting apart along the long, narrow gash of the Red Sea, which runs between the Arabian Desert and Northern Africa. The gaps between Africa and Eurasia began opening 35 million years ago along the 1,600-mile (2,560 km) Red Sea, splitting the Middle East from Africa. This rift has played a vital role in spawning three of the world's religions and perhaps the human species itself.

Many geophysicists maintain that the Red Sea is really a young ocean, which will one day form a new basin to rival the Atlantic Ocean. The Red Sea is merely the deepest, wettest part of a system of rifts that will eventually rip loose a huge chunk of Eastern Africa, perhaps casting it adrift as a minicontinent like Australia. Geologists think that the ridge emerging under the Red Sea will split into a system of ridges dividing at least three different crustal plates. That will eventually create an ocean ridge running down Africa's Great Rift Valley.

Such rifts on the seafloor have created the Earth's terrain and ultimately control the distribution of deserts. The movement of continents embedded in crustal plates explains why a piece of land can move from junglelike conditions near the equator to areas where dry descending air creates deserts. The *rift system* that promises to eventually move the Arabian Desert once again runs for nearly 4,000 miles (6,400 km) from Syria through the Sea of Galilee, into the Gulf of Aqaba and the Red Sea and then on down Africa, where it splits into two rift systems. The rifted slump in the crust is marked in Africa by a series of mountains, like Mount Kilimanjaro, and deep troughs, like the ones that hold 4,500-foot-deep (1,500 m) Lake Tanganyika and Lake Victoria, the second largest freshwater lake in the world.

In the low-lying deserts of these rift valleys, archaeologists have found the bones of our earliest ancestors, including the 3-million-year-old skeleton of Lucy. Experts on human evolution now believe that several types of big-brained hominids lived in the forests and savannas of east Africa. From there, they spread outward across the other continents, probably passing along the shores of the Red Sea.

ARABIAN PENINSULA NOURISHED CIVILIZATION

Oddly enough, the same titanic forces that created the Arabian Desert at the head of this great rift system also nurtured the rise of Western civilizations and three of the world's dominant religions. North of the Red Sea, the Suez Canal connects directly to the Mediterranean Sea, which is shrinking as a result of the same movements that are opening up the Red Sea and shifting the Arabian Peninsula north. Eventually, Africa will slowly rotate and plow into Europe.

The unexpected side effects of the titanic forces that ripped the Middle East loose from Africa have sustained civilization. The split drove Arabia into Asia, pushing the small, dwindling Arabian plate down underneath Asia. The result was a huge, sallow sea. These shallow coastal waters provided the perfect home for plankton, algae, and other creatures that drifted and floated in the sunlit waters. When they died, their bodies sunk to the bottom, creating layers of mud rich in organic debris, along with the mud and rock washing in from the surrounding landmasses. This went on for millions of years. Periodically, the climate would shift due to small variations in the wobble of the Earth's orbit around the sun. During cold ice ages, the oceans would drop as huge quantities of water accumulated as snow and ice at the Poles. During warm periods, the polar ice would melt and the sea levels would rise. As a result, the ocean repeatedly invaded the shallow basin. When climate shifted and the ocean fell, it would leave behind a stranded, shallow sea that would eventually evaporate, leaving a thick layer of salt. Eventually, these salt layers sealed up the sediment trapped in the bottom of the basin.

Those buried mud layers laced with the remains of microscopic sea creatures plus the organic debris of the marshes and swamps that dominated the sunken area when the ocean retreated were capped by layers of salt and other sediment, trapping them in place deep beneath the surface. There, thousands of feet beneath the surface, the heat and pressure gradually transformed these buried organic deposits into oil and natural gas. This oil remained trapped by the cap of salt and sediment as the heat-

THE ARABIAN HORSE

The oldest purebred horse, the magnificent Arabian, which starred in *The Black Stallion*, has played a key role in human history and the development of our intimate relationship with the horse. Distinguished by their narrow, delicate faces with large nostrils and a teacup muzzle, the Arabian's lineage dates back to at least 1500 B.C. It played a key role in the survival of the *Bedouin* tribes, who often swept out of the desert to raid more settled people. The Bedouins also wagered vast sums on horse races, which played a crucial cultural and economic role. The Arabian became the mainstay of a succession of empires stretching back some 3,500 years, including the Egyptians, Hurrians, Hittites, Kassites, Assyrians, Babylonians, and Persians. The prophet Mohammed in A.D. 600 was talking about the Arabian when he taught that "every man shall love his horse." And the grace and character of the breed totally charmed Napoléon Bonaparte when he invaded the Middle East in 1798.

ing caused it to expand and press against the unyielding cap of sediment. As a result, when geologists eventually drilled holes to penetrate these caps, the oil expanded into the pipes and drill holes to create oil gushers. The result was the vast oil fields of the Middle East that have fueled the world's economy and a succession of wars that have plagued the region in the past century.

The Arabian Desert harbors the world's largest single oil field, Ghawar, which is 174 miles (278 km) long and 16 miles (27 km) wide and contains an estimated 55 billion barrels of oil. Every day, oil companies pump out 5 million barrels, which makes the area vital to the economy of the gasoline-addicted world. Ghawar's oil is contained in 280-foot-thick (93 m) layers of limestone laid down in the late Jurassic period, but now some 7,000 feet (2,134 m) below the surface. A bulging anticline of anhydrite rock lies on top of the Ghawar limestones, trapping and pressurizing the oil beneath. Initially, the oil gushed from the wells under its own pressure, but as the oil companies pumped out more and more oil they had to start injecting millions of gallons of pressurized water back into the limestone layer to keep up the pressure. In addition, energy companies extract another 2 billion cubic feet of natural gas every day, mostly from *shales* 14,000 feet (4,700 m) beneath the surface. These shales were laid down in marshes and sea bottoms during the Silurian period, between 443 and 417 million years ago. At this time, Earth's climate warmed and stabilized, which melted much of the ice cap at either pole. Seas rose and flooded what would one day become the Arabian Desert, which led to the formation of the organic-rich shales on the seafloor. At about the same time, the first coral reefs developed and fish underwent major changes. The first fish with jaws emerged, as did the first freshwater fish.

HIDDEN RICHES OF THE ARABIAN DESERT

That long, rich geologic history helps explain the vital importance to the world of this seemingly barren and inhospitable desert. In its northern reaches, the 1,300-mile-long (2,080 km) Arabian Peninsula merges with Arab Asia through the treeless plains of Syria. The highest point lies in Yemen, 12,336-foot (3,760 m) Mount Al-Nabi Shu'ayb. Much of the peninsula is low, dry, and hot, but the southern tip is dominated by the Yemen plateau, with an average elevation of 7,000 feet (2,100 m).

West of the Red Sea the area is bounded by a remarkable line of 2,000-foot-tall (670 m) cliffs that run for some 600 miles (960 km). Caused by a massive uplift of the Earth due to the rifting along the bottom of the Red Sea, the elevation changes from some 600 feet (670 m) at the base of this uplifted line of cliffs to some 3,300 feet (1,100 m) along their lip. These rugged cliffs cut off the desert interior from moist ocean air and have long isolated the distinctive desert people who have made a hard living here for thousands of years. Great sandy, rocky plains with only modest hills mark the rest of the Arabian Desert. Nearly featureless expanses of sand cover perhaps one-third of the total area.

This whole landscape is laid down on top of one of Earth's most remarkable geological features, the African Shield, a mass of Precambrian gneiss that includes rocks formed some 2.6 billion years ago as a great, molten mass deep beneath the surface. Shifts in the Earth have forced this molten mass of rock to the surface in the past 500 to 900 million years, determining the foundation geology of much of Africa.

The final major stage in creating the current landscape began some 35 million years ago when the Red Sea began to open up along this deep crack in the Earth. This created a titanic series of volcanic outbursts some 20 to 30 million years ago. Magma broke through fractures in the rifting crust and burst out onto the surface. In some places, the flood of molten *basalts* piled on in layers up to 9,800 feet (3,000 m) thick. These almost unimaginable lava floods now form the mountains along the Red Sea margin in Yemen. A second, much smaller volcanic period ended about 10,000 years ago, leaving lava domes and an extensive fault system along the western edge of the desert. Some 18 relatively young volcanic fields are scattered throughout the area, some of them covering 10,000 square miles (25,899 sq km).

The same forces that created these volcanic outbreaks have left several large, uplifted plateaus. That includes most of Jordan east of the Dead Sea, the sandstone mass of Mount Al-Tubayq in the southeast, and several other plateaus that advance to the edge of the Al-Nafud, the great sand desert of the north.

A LANDSCAPE OF SAND

The great, flat sandy plains separating both the volcanic mountain ranges and the uplifted plateaus dominate most of the Arabian Desert. Covered with rocks or gravel fitted into something of an armor plating by the patient actions of wind and frost, these desert pavement surfaces protect the dry, sandy soil beneath. Some of the plains are covered with a salt-based crust known as duricrusted soil. This salty crust also prevents the frequent winds from picking up the dry sand that is largely unanchored by plant roots. Other areas are dominated by gravel plains, covered with interlocking pebbles and chips of chert washed down onto the plains during the wet Pleistocene epoch (1.8 million to 10,000 years ago). Only dry washes that hold water during the rare storms remain in this desert, but these wadis follow the ghostly path of great rivers that flowed during the ice ages, when this desert was a grassy plain with scattered trees much

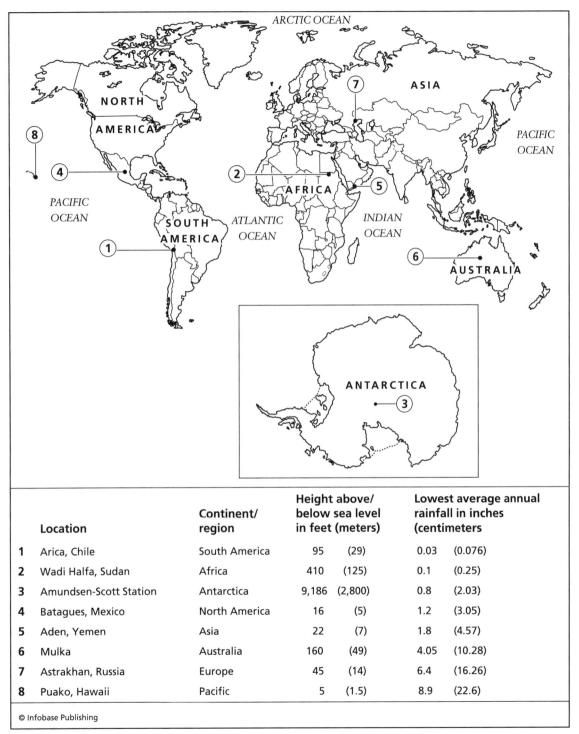

	Location	Continent/region	Height above/below sea level in feet (meters)		Lowest average annual rainfall in inches (centimeters)	
1	Arica, Chile	South America	95	(29)	0.03	(0.076)
2	Wadi Halfa, Sudan	Africa	410	(125)	0.1	(0.25)
3	Amundsen-Scott Station	Antarctica	9,186	(2,800)	0.8	(2.03)
4	Batagues, Mexico	North America	16	(5)	1.2	(3.05)
5	Aden, Yemen	Asia	22	(7)	1.8	(4.57)
6	Mulka	Australia	160	(49)	4.05	(10.28)
7	Astrakhan, Russia	Europe	45	(14)	6.4	(16.26)
8	Puako, Hawaii	Pacific	5	(1.5)	8.9	(22.6)

© Infobase Publishing

World's driest places

like the areas of southern Africa where scientists believe our ancestors evolved following great herds of animals. Several of the river deltas left by these vanished systems are as large as the current delta of the Nile River. These traces of vanished rivers testify to the startling realization that most of the deserts of the world are surprisingly young, including this one surrounding the cradle of civilization.

Today, this network of dry wadis is just a ghostly memory of those great river systems, but they remain vital to the history and ecology of the Arabian Desert. Only one of the region's drainage systems carries water year-round, the network of wadis and tributaries that feed into the Tigris and Euphrates rivers and the Wadi Hajr in the south.

The region also has some strange geological features, like the sabkhah, or saline flat, that forms along the coast where the repeated advance and evaporation of the sea has left a concentration of salty, mineralized brine just below the surface. This salty crust reaches a thickness of perhaps three feet (1 m), interlaced with layers of mud and other sediments like gypsum. An innocent-looking layer of sand may cover these dangerous layers of salty slush. But an unwary traveler can suddenly break through this thin crust of normal sand and find himself floundering in deep layers of gooey, silty muck with the consistency of custard.

The desert also harbors great dune fields, which come in every shape and size and form a complex, constantly shifting topography. One dune field in the Al-Nafud covers 25,000 square miles (65,000 sq km). An even larger dune field, the Rub' al-Khali, covers 250,000 square miles (650,000 sq km). Some of these dunes reach heights of 300 feet (91.4 m), high enough to bury a typical American city without leaving a trace. Some of those dunes take forms unique to the Arabian Desert, including a giant crescent-shaped dune with a steep slope that moves constantly, with a hollow in the arms of the crescent that reaches bedrock so that from the air the dune looks like a giant hoof.

The single most barren and desolate area is called Rub' al-Khali, the Empty Quarter. It covers an area larger than France in the southern part of Saudi Arabia and over into the borders of Oman and Yemen. Even the desert-dwelling Bedouins, whose caravan routes have crisscrossed this desert for centuries, rarely venture into the waterless Rub' al-Khali.

FOR DESERTS—
LOCATION, LOCATION, LOCATION

Sprawling along 22° of latitude, most of the Arabian Desert lies north of the tropic of Cancer. Summer heat reaches temperatures of 129°F (54°C). Although some of the coastal stretches get moisture in the form of ocean fogs at night and in the morning, most of the sandy expanse gets less than 4 inches (100 mm) of rain annually. However, some areas can get up to 20 inches (500 mm) in a wet year and then go for several years without a drop. The desert cools significantly in the winter, particularly on some of the high plateaus and mountain ranges. The coldest temperature recorded was in 1950, about 10°F (–12°C). That cold snap resulted in a dramatically rare dusting of snow.

Strong winds lash the desert, especially in January to December and May to June. These *shamals* usually blow down along the desert from the north, sometimes steadily at 30 miles an hour for a full month. Utterly dry, the winds move millions of tons of sand in every storm. They spawn whirlwinds called *jinn* and merciless storms that make it nearly impossible to travel for days at a time. Sometimes storm fronts called "brown rollers" march along on an opaque front of 60 miles (96 km) or more, swirling dust high into the atmosphere and bringing rain in their wake.

PLANTS COPE WITH SALT AND HEAT

Surviving in such a harsh, hot, waterless place demands special adaptations in desert plants. Most have made elaborate adjustments to the lack of water. Many are halophytic, or salt tolerant, having evolved ways to handle loads of salt and minerals that would kill most plants. Many of the low-lying areas into which the wadis drain are former lakebeds, and the soil is laced with the salts and minerals left behind by evaporating water.

Tough seeds of frail annuals and grasses lie scattered in the soil, often waiting for years for a single wet year so they can blossom. Sometimes during a wet spring, the seemingly barren reaches of the desert suddenly sprout a green fuzz of wildflowers. Herders like the Bedouins have relied on such fitful bounty to graze their sheep, camels, and the famed Arabian horse. But centuries of overuse have generally overtaxed the grasses and flowers, leading to a steady expansion in the areas now virtually devoid of plant life.

Other plants have adjusted in surprising ways. The tamarisk tree grows near the scattered oases. It puts roots down deep to reach the water table and sports tough, scratchy threadlike leaves that gather in the Sun's energy with a minimum loss of moisture. These trees were so tough in a harsh environment that they were imported into the American Southwest to serve as windbreaks to protect railroad tracks. They quickly spread and are now one of the major pest species in the American Southwest, especially in riparian areas already hard hit by cattle grazing, dams, and water pumping. Tamarisks have largely replaced native cottonwoods and willows along thousands of miles of waterways in the American deserts.

Some of the most historically important plants are modest shrubs and trees that produce resins used to make frankincense and myrrh, precious species the wise men reportedly brought as gifts to the newborn Jesus. The fragrance was used extensively for ceremonies, religious rituals, cremations, and royal processions. For centuries, these prized fragrances drove a rich trade network. One recent study using satellite images has mapped the faint shadow of a lost civilization in the Empty Quarter in Oman, using infrared imagery to detect a network of ancient roads beneath hundreds of feet of sand. Scientists believe that the ghostly network of roads and ruins marks the location of the lost civilization of Ad, which grew wealthy and powerful by gathering and then selling frankincense some 5,000 years ago. Brave but frustrated explorers spent years searching for the seemingly mythical civilization of Ad. But the hardships of the Empty Quarter and the massive, shifting sand dunes frustrated every effort. However, the images from the satellites revealed the traces of a 100-yard-wide (91.4 m), hoof-trodden path beneath giant sand dunes, the trade route along which the horse and camel caravans distributed frankincense to the world. The city of Ubar, the Atlantis of the Sands as adventurer T. E. Lawrence dubbed it, was probably the main center in the frankincense trade from about 3000 B.C. to the first century A.D. The Bible, the Koran, and the folktales of the Arabian Nights all mention Ubar.

Another vital plant of the Arabian Desert is the date palm, which grows in the handful of oases where water trapped beneath the surface thousands of years ago bubbles to the surface due to some quirk of the underground rock formations. The date palm and these widely spaced oases formed the basis of life for many desert people. The palm provided wood for building and making well frames, its fronds covered their roofs and its rich, nutritious fruit was a mainstay in their diets. The desert people also grew a variety of other crops close to the oases, including citrus, melons, onions, peaches, grapes, wheat, and even prickly pears, this last an import from North America since the Arabian Desert has no native cactus species.

STRANGE ANIMALS THRIVE IN HARSH CONDITIONS

Many of the most unique and specially adapted creatures of the Arabian Desert have already disappeared or cling to a rootlet of survival. One remarkable creature that has vanished from most of the desert is the ferocious honey badger, a 10-inch-long (250 mm), 25-pound (11 kg) mass of muscle and aggression also known as the ratel. Armed with a thick skull, powerful muscles, and massive claws used for digging and excavating, the ratel has loose skin around its neck so thick that even leopards have a hard time biting through. The ratels have a nasty habit of charging and trying to rip out the groin of their opponents, which has enabled them to kill even adult buffalo, wildebeest, and waterbuck. They have reportedly chased young lions away from their kills and are thought to be immune to many varieties of snake venom.

Ratels will eat anything they can catch, but are especially fond of bees and honey. They have formed a strange partnership with small birds called honeyguides. These birds flit up to ratels and get their attention by singing and flashing a bold display with white marking on their wings. The bird will then lead the ratel to a beehive, as the ratel answers the bird's distinctive song with a low growl. Once the ratel reaches the hive, he sprays it with a suffocating secretion from his anus gland, which causes the bees outside the hive to flee and stuns or kills those remaining inside. The ratel then breaks open the hive and devours the honey and the dead bees. The honeyguide waits his turn impatiently, then flits in and dines on dead and stunned bees.

THE SHIP OF THE DESERT: THE CAMEL

The camel remains one of the most remarkable and important of all desert-adapted animals. Consider the following facts about the camel:

- Go seven months without drinking, if they can get moisture in their food
- Go two weeks without a drink even if they eat nothing in the heat of summer
- Lose 40 percent of its body weight to dehydration without ill effect (humans die if they lose 12 percent)
- Avoid the effects of dehydration because their oval blood cells do not stick together when their blood thickens
- Drink 28 gallons (127 liters) of water at one sitting or 45 gallons (204 liters) in one 24-hour period
- Guzzle water at a rate of up to 7 gallons (32 l) a minute
- Withstand a body temperature of 107°F (42°C) that would kill a human being
- Withstand both heat and cold because their fur provides such great insulation that even snowflakes will not melt on it
- Run at 40 miles (64 km) per hour
- Carry 770 pounds (349 kg) a distance of 278 miles (445 km) in 16 days
- Carry up to 1,907 (864 kg) pounds at a time
- Ignore sandstorms due to a transparent eyelid
- Filter out dust and avoid losing moisture thanks to an intricate, hair-lined sinus cavity
- Make a squeaking sound to attract female camels by grinding its teeth

Another remarkable but endangered creature of the Arabian Desert is the Arabian oryx, a white antelope with striking black markings on its face and dark legs. The oryx may have given rise to the myth of the unicorn, since its long, twin, gently-curving horns often look like a single horn from the side. Once abundant throughout the Arabian Peninsula, hunters wiped them out in the decades after the introduction of guns and cars that could cross the vast expanse of sand. A few survivors retreated into the Empty Quarter, where they somehow survived in a place too wild and harsh for hunters. Before hunters turned them into trophies, the oryx had spawned generations of myth and legend. That started with a 13th-century account by a Frenchman of the legend of the unicorn and the virgin. The supposedly fierce unicorn could not be captured unless it laid its head in the lap of a virgin. Arab poets also wrote many poems comparing the grace of the oryx to a beautiful woman. The Bedouin believed that in capturing or killing an oryx they could claim its qualities of strength and endurance.

In fact, the exquisitely adapted oryx can live for years without drinking, gleaning all the moisture it needs from the plants it eats and from nibbling at plants graced by early morning dew. The oryx has an astonishing ability to extract every last molecule of water from its food and then endlessly recycle that water through its kidneys. The oryx thrives on tough, dry plants, even many with defensive chemicals that deter most other animals. When it does rain, the oryx can somehow sense the storm when it is still over the horizon and move quickly to intercept its path.

The oryx had disappeared from the wild by 1972. Fortunately, a few animals survived in captivity and the Phoenix Zoo and others undertook a captive breeding program. As a result, a small herd has now been released back into the wild.

It seems fitting to make such an effort to return one of the most brilliantly adapted creatures to this great desert. After all, the hard lessons of these desert sands gave rise to Western civilization, so it seems only fair we should give the oryx back.

7

Kalahari Desert

Southern Africa

Odds are, human beings hit upon the lifestyle and innovations that enabled them to populate the planet in some place very like the Kalahari Desert, a small, surprisingly diverse, just-barely desert in southern Africa that still harbors what many geneticists consider the original human beings. The 100,000-square-mile (260,000 sq km) Kalahari is a faint echo of the vast Sahara Desert. The Kalahari is a desert for two reasons. First, it is just as far south of the equator as the Sahara is north, which means that it is a Southern Hemisphere desert for the same reason that the Sahara is a Northern Hemisphere desert and subject to the same drying, descending winds. Second, the Kalahari sits on a plateau about 3,000 feet above sea level and is bounded by mountains to the north and south, which cast a long rain shadow.

The Kalahari occupies central and southwestern Botswana, part of west central South Africa and part of eastern Namibia. It is part of a vast 360,000-square-mile (930,000 sq km) sand basin that stretches into Angola and Zambia in the north and takes in much of South Africa and Namibia. This larger region has great dune fields that have been frozen into place by a covering of plants, which indicates that it is part of a fossil desert. At some point it converted from true desert to arid grasslands as a result of climate shifts. A Southern Hemisphere desert with seasons reversed from the Northern Hemisphere, temperatures range from 95 to 113°F (35–45°C) in the hot months from October to March and often drop below freezing in the winter months of June to August.

The Kalahari Desert has a pronounced rainy season at the north end, but dries out into a true desert toward the south. Its flat, rolling topography, life-giving rainy season, great expanses of grass, varied vegetation, and sharp climate difference between north and south make the Kalahari one of the richest of desert habitats, rivaled only by North America's Sonoran Desert. This ecological variety might also account for the crucial role the region has played in human evolution.

Kalahari Desert

For at least 30,000 years, the San, or Bushmen as they call themselves, have occupied this demanding landscape. Geneticists attempting to reconstruct human evolution believe that the Bushmen may represent the original human stock, since all other human groups show a genetic connection to the Bushmen that suggests all those other groups have evolved away from these founders of the human line. The genetic evidence suggests that sometime in the last 100,000 years, human beings moved out of Africa and populated the planet. The ancestors of the Bushmen who remained behind in Africa therefore represent the original genetic stock, since they remained isolated in the Kalahari with only minimal genetic mixing with other groups. Moreover, the Kalahari Kung San Bushmen developed a remarkably stable culture that adapted to the hard conditions of their desert-savannah environment through an intimate knowledge of the land rather than technology.

The rich assemblage of other creatures that take advantage of the climatic and ecological diversity of the Kalahari might also provide insight into how human beings developed an adaptable culture that made it possible for people to spread out of Africa and make a living on every continent. The difference between the north and south and the bounty of the wet season in the north prompts great migrations of an array of animals, including elephants, antelope, giraffes, warthogs, hyenas, jackals, lions, bat-eared foxes, and even the rare wild dog, perhaps the ancestor of all domesticated dogs.

This diversity makes the Kalahari Desert essential to understanding the evolution of human beings and our relationship to the land and to other creatures. Moreover, the Kalahari is in the midst of wrenching ecological changes that stem directly from human activities—which makes it both the nursery of the human species and now a test of humanity's maturity.

THE ORIGINAL PEOPLE

Once upon a time, paleontologists believed that human beings and the other primates went their separate ways 15 to 30 million years ago. They based the conclusion on inexact and wide-ranging dating of bits of teeth and skulls scattered throughout the world. Moreover, paleontologists found bits and pieces of big-brained, upright-walking hominids they believed gave rise to modern humans in sites throughout Asia and Europe. Scientists in the early 20th century therefore concluded that the ancestors of modern humans had spread across much of Eurasia and Africa millions of years ago. These distinct, local populations might then have mingled to form the stock for modern humans.

But some 30 years ago, scientists with new research and new ideas challenged the conclusions of the fossil hunters. The new work was based on a careful analysis of the genetic blueprint coded into the spiral of *DNA*. Every cell contains a coil of DNA in its nucleus. This coil of *amino acids* contains the instructions for making all of the complex proteins that comprise the cell and enable it to carry out its business. Initially, geneticists thought human beings had about 100,000 genes, but recent work has reduced the number of actual genes to about 30,000. Living species change and evolve largely because of changes in their DNA. Any genetically based characteristic that helps a person, bacteria, or elephant leave more children will tend to spread through the population.

But while the 30,000 functioning human genes are therefore subjected to this continual pruning and selective pressure, many stretches along that DNA spiral are just accumulated random junk, no longer functioning as genes and therefore no longer pruned and discarded by the process of genetic evolution. These noncoding pieces of DNA therefore accumulate without changing as much as the actively evolving genes. Geneticists sought to take advantage of that fact by using these randomly accumulated genetic bits to compare one species to another. Moreover, elaborate experiments revealed that these random, noncoding bits accumulate at a fairly constant rate over the course of hundreds of thousands of years, which means they can be used as a molecular clock.

This discovery opened the door to a scientific revolution. Geneticists discovered they could directly compare the DNA of any group of creatures, compare the accumulation of these random bits, and get a rough idea as to the last time those two species had identical DNA, which would indicate when they last shared a common ancestor.

These scientific innovators compared the DNA of human beings to their nearest relatives, chimpanzees and gorillas. To their surprise, the DNA-based molecular clock suggested that human beings, chimpanzees, and gorillas all shared a common ancestor as recently as 5 to 7 million years ago. In fact, humans, chimpanzees, and gorillas share about 98 to 99 percent of the same genes.

Another equally startling discovery soon followed. Human beings are almost genetically identical to one another, at least as compared to other species. Despite the apparently significant differences in appearance between different human populations and races, the genetic differences between various groups are tiny. Two different subspecies of seemingly identical sparrows actually have much greater genetic differences than, say, Native Americans and Europeans. That finding suggests that all current human populations shared a common ancestor in the recent past.

So researchers gathered DNA samples from virtually every human population in the world. They then set out to compare all these coils of DNA. Seeking a way to make the analysis easier, they focused on a curious little cell-within-a-cell, the mitochondria. Modern cells probably represent an alliance long ago between two microscopic organisms, the ancestor of the cell and the ancestor of the mitochondria. Now, every cell uses this strange structure to essentially produce the energy it needs. Oddly enough, the mitochondria floating around inside the much larger cell has its own microscopic coil of DNA, a sign of its once-independent existence. But the *mitochondrial* DNA comes only from the mother's egg, which means it does not split and take half of its DNA from the sperm cell of the father like the main coil of DNA in the cell. Therefore, the DNA in the mitochondria gets shuffled and reshuffled much less often than the DNA in the main part of the cell. That makes the mitochondrial DNA perfect for charting the random accumulation of mutations that makes the molecular clock analysis possible.

The comparison of human mitochondrial DNA yielded some remarkable findings. First, all human beings living today are descended from the same woman who may have lived as recently as 70,000 years ago, although some studies put the date at 120,000 to 180,000 years ago. Moreover, if you charted the variation between all the different human groups, the Bushmen of the Kalahari sit right in the middle, indicating that all other groups are equally related to the Bushmen. This suggests that the DNA of the Bushmen is closest to the root of the human family tree. That conclusion also matches the fossil evidence. Therefore, most experts now believe that modern human beings evolved on the semiarid desert plains of Africa and spread throughout the world from there.

STUDYING THE HUMAN MYSTERY

Thus, the lifestyle of the Bushmen who have lived in balance with the demands of the desert grasslands of the Kalahari for at least 30,000 years may provide invaluable clues to human origins and our original hunter-gatherer lifestyle. The traditional Bushmen were renowned for an intimate knowledge of the desert that enabled them to make use of every plant and animal. They made an array of effective medicines from plants, often taking advantage of the chemicals plants produce to protect themselves from insects, fungi, and bacteria. They also learned to make a variety of poisons, which enabled them to successfully hunt even elephants using bows and spears. They apparently mastered the same skills as the Ice Age big game hunters that may have played a role in the extinction of creatures like mammoths, giant ground sloths, and other mega-fauna in places like Europe, North America, and even Australia.

The Bushmen were famed for their legendary endurance, since they could go long periods without water and run at a steady jog for days at a time. This lean, relentless conditioning and long-range endurance enabled them to undertake long-ranging hunts. If they wounded an antelope with a poisoned arrow, they could run for hours and many miles along the track of the wounded animal, waiting for the slow-acting poison to bring the creature down. Moreover, the traditional Bushmen displayed amazing powers of tracking and observation. They could read the tracks from a broken twig or a faint indentation. They could use the traces and tracks of the animals they hunted to figure out what they were eating, where they were going, and their age. They often could anticipate storms and shifts in the weather, locate water from the faintest traces, insightfully interpret animal behavior, and thrive in places that would prompt most other people to wander in desperate, dehydrated circles.

Generally, they lived a restless, nomadic lifestyle, taking advantage of their simple technology and mere tracery of possessions to move easily over great distances to follow the migrations of animals and the temporary flowering of resources in one area or another. They developed certain claimed areas, but often moved in and out of those areas with the seasonal resources. Some groups lived for generations in caves in Drakensberg and elsewhere. In that area, clans also inherited rights to tend to and harvest honey nests and certain territories where they could dig for grubs, the larva of certain insects that hollow out and live in roots of various trees.

The Bushmen also made effective use of desert termites, who make up for the lack of wood and moist topsoil by using mud and secretions to build cementlike, raised mounds that sometimes stand five or six feet tall. Biologists calculate that if you combined all the termites in the world, they'd outweigh the human beings. Certainly, the termites play a crucial role in breaking down wood fiber and recycling their nutrients into the soil. Safe in humid, brilliantly constructed, and ventilated aboveground nests, the termite mounds sometimes create bizarre, alien landscapes. The Bushmen learned how to harvest termites and their nutrient-rich grubs, which they fry up like popcorn or pound into tasty snacks, without destroying the termite mound. As a result, the rights to certain mounds

THE BUSHMAN DIET DRUG

Ironically, the wisdom of their traditional culture may harbor treasures that could mitigate their otherwise brutal poverty. For instance, the San Bushmen have long chewed pieces of the hoodia cactus to take the edge off hunger, since they sometimes had to go days with little or nothing to eat on long hunts or in times of drought. South African scientists were testing the plant based on Bushman accounts of its usefulness when they isolated an unknown molecule they named P57. The substance has exceptional promise as an appetite suppressant, which could ironically enough reduce one of the 21st century's great scourges—obesity.

Apparently, brain cells that constitute the *hypothalamus* play a key role in sensing glucose sugar levels in the blood. The glucose levels in the bloodstream rise during and after meals, which eventually prompt certain brain cells in the hypothalamus to respond. That makes a person feel full, so they stop eating. The substance produced by hoodia serves some still-unknown function in the squat, bristly, mutated-looking cactus, but in the human bloodstream it apparently mimics glucose, except it is 10,000 times as active. As a result, the brain quickly gets that full feeling, and people who take the substance lose their appetites. The substance prompts normally gluttonous rats to stop eating entirely. In an experiment with overweight human volunteers, people taking the substance reduced their food intake by 1,000 calories a day without even noticing. Although scientists must still determine whether the substance has any unexpected side effects, it is possible that a substance that the direct descendants of the first humans used to cope with near-starvation will save many others from death by obesity. Fortunately, the researchers agreed to a patent and royalty arrangement with representatives of the Bushmen, so if the drug is a huge success it may actually benefit the Bushmen.

are passed along in a single family or clan and jealously protected from outsiders.

The Bushmen lived in loose family bands that combined and split apart as resources and personalities dictated. They had no police, no justice system, and a social system that gives each individual great freedom but essential obligations to their immediate and extended family. The harsh conditions sometimes enforced a hard morality on them, and it was not unusual for a woman with a nursing baby to be compelled to abandon a newborn in times of drought or famine.

Unfortunately, like many native peoples, the Bushmen are increasingly hard pressed to preserve even shreds of their traditional lifestyle. Isolated for thousands of years by the rigors of the desert to which they were so well adapted, they first came under pressure from outside groups when cattle-herding, Bantu-speaking Twsana, Kgalagadi, and Herero people arrived from the north and south in the 1800s. They generally pushed the Khoisan-speaking Bushmen into the more desertlike areas and claimed the seasonally watered grasslands for their livestock.

A small number of European settlers arrived a short time later, ultimately bringing additional wrenching changes to the Bushmen. Initially, the Europeans avoided the driest part of the desert. When the Boers crossed the Kalahari in 1878, 250 people and some 9,000 cattle died in the crossing. But they soon occupied the areas with grass and water. Generally the Bushmen living in the better-watered regions quickly succumbed to disease, absorption, and outright genocide. That left a dwindling number of Bushmen living in the deep desert. Many of the survivors took up cattle raising and assimilated into the developing modern culture. Today, only an estimated 5 percent of the Bushmen still live in the desert in a traditional way. A total of about 100,000 San Bushmen remain alive anywhere.

A FOSSIL DESERT

In many ways, the Kalahari is more of a fossil desert than an actual desert. The great sand-covered plateau that includes the Kalahari is testament to desert conditions that once more closely resembled the Sahara than the current *semiarid* grassland mitigated by scattered acacia trees and shrubs, which fill the same niche that plants like mesquite do in the deserts of North America. The region is marked by massive sand dunes, generally running north-south and ranging in height from 20 to 200 feet (6–61 m). The dunes run parallel for 50 miles (80.5 km) or more, creating ridges separated by intervening channels. Such sand dunes in the Sahara to the north are actively growing and shifting, so that no plants can get rooted before they are buried by the shift of the dune. The Kalahari must have been built up under similar conditions, but at some point rainfall patterns shifted sufficiently that the winds pushing the dune moderated and the plants got enough water to put down roots and stabilize the dune surface. Therefore, the dunes of the Kalahari are now long, stable, grass- and shrub-covered ridgelines.

The dunes stabilized some 10,000 to 20,000 years ago, for reasons climate scientists do not fully understand. Curiously, while the end of the last ice age some 10,000 years ago created many of the modern deserts, in the Kalahari it apparently moderated desert conditions. That massive climate shift made conditions much more harsh in the Sahara and in North America turned grasslands into deserts. But here, the same shift apparently converted a raw sand desert into a semiarid grassland. The explanation probably lies in planetwide shifts in rainfall patterns relating to the accompanying warming, sea level rise, and shifts in trade winds, ocean temperatures, and monsoons. Although the Kalahari remained in a desert-prone latitude hedged in by rain-blocking mountains, enough of an enhanced wet season delivered plenty of rain to greatly soften the desert conditions.

As in most deserts, water remains the crucial limiting factor. The Kalahari receives an average of about 8 inches (203.2 mm) of rain per year, while the surrounding semiarid sand plains receive far more. Even so, the rain remains variable and seasonal, with some years yielding two or three times the annual average.

Most of the year, not a single stream, river, lake, or pond breaks the desert surface. The only permanent surface water is the Boteti River, flowing out of the great swamps of the Okavango delta at the northern edge of the desert in northern Botswana. Here, hippos and a variety of aquatic birds and animals provide a rich resource. Heavy rains throughout the desert can cause periodic floods, but dry stream channels quickly deliver the floodwaters to flat low-lying depressions with no outlet. The water collects into shallow, fleeting lakes before evaporating and leaving behind dissolved salts and minerals. As a result, these low-lying salt flats or pans resemble the same features found in almost all deserts.

Several lakes on the edge of the desert, including Lake Xau and Lake Ngami also sometimes collect the floodwaters that heavy storms send crashing through the Kalahari, as well as the flow of the Boteti River, much of which is carried underground. The lack of permanent water means the Kalahari has only a handful of native fish species, but that includes the remarkable Brooder Fish, which compensates for the hard and uncertain times by keeping its eggs in its mouth until they hatch, whereupon the mother tenderly spits her hatchlings out into an uncertain world.

GREAT ANIMAL MIGRATIONS

Any creatures that live in the Kalahari must therefore either survive without relying on easy access to surface water or migrate through the area during the times when the scarce rains fall. Perhaps the most distinctive feature of the Kalahari is the way in which it blends into the larger, surrounding stretch of arid grasslands, which accounts for the remarkable migrations of game animals through and around the desert. This migration and the human reaction to it may help explain the cultural and environmental shifts that helped human beings spread out of Africa and populate the globe perhaps as recently as 70,000 years ago.

One of the most striking, seasonal, migratory residents of the region is the African elephant. The adult males stand 10 feet (3.05 m) tall at the shoulder and weigh up to six tons. They have life spans of 70 years and a crucial and intimate social structure. During much of the year, the females and the young keep to themselves, all responding to the leadership of a dominant female. During the breeding season, dominant males gather up harems. Experiments have shown that young male elephants learn how to behave from the dominant male elephant. If poachers or accidents kill off the patriarch and the young males are raised in a group without a dominant male, they will become the elephant equivalent of juvenile delinquents who get into fights, destroy farmland, knock down houses, and generally misbehave. The elephants mostly migrate through the Kalahari during wet seasons when they can find water temporarily collected in the pans or salt flats.

The Kalahari also boasts a great variety of antelope species, perhaps because these fleet, hardy, wary creatures are well adapted to desert conditions. Most antelope have hardy dispositions and remarkable

WEAVERBIRD COMMUNES

One of the most remarkable creatures of the Kalahari Desert is the sparrowlike weaverbird. Small, gray creatures, they are unremarkable unless they have gathered in a group, when they become one of the planet's most interesting and sociable birds. Hundreds of birds form a single flock, which then cooperatively weaves a giant nest of twigs that can all but absorb an acacia tree, especially the viciously barbed camelthorn tree. These acacia trees provide one of the few refuges for birds in the heart of the Kalahari, since the trees can withstand 10 months without a drop of rain. The nests can measure six feet (1.83 m) or more across and provide refuge for hundreds of birds.

By some calculation known only to weaverbirds, they allocate annual nesting rights. Some percentage of the females lay eggs while the other, nonbreeding members of the colony cooperate to feed the nesting parents and their offspring.

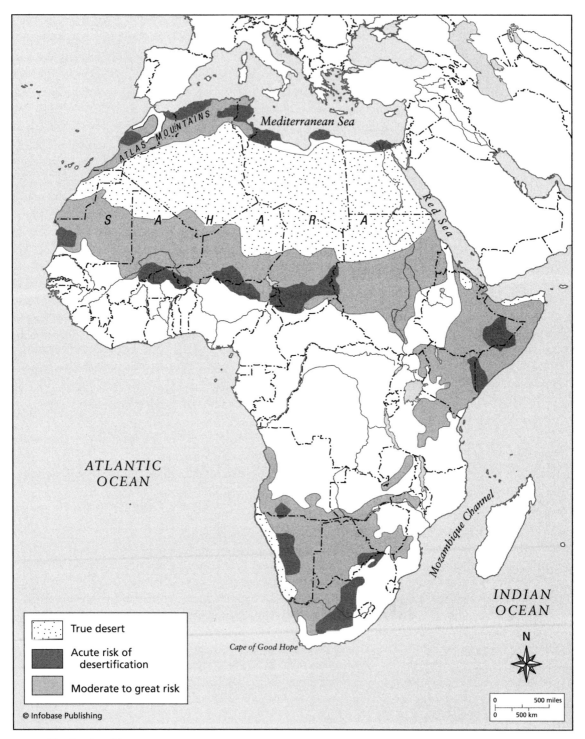

Desertification in Africa

metabolisms that allow them to withstand greater heat and make prolonged physical exertions, even in desert heat that would quickly debilitate most other hoofed animals. Moreover, most antelope are blessed with tough, efficient kidneys that enable them to withstand otherwise lethal dehydration and to extract most of the moisture they need from their food.

As a result of their adaptation to the desert, many species of antelope and their close relatives roam the Kalahari. The antelope have sustained the Bushmen for 30,000 years and may have provided a food source and a nomadic lifestyle for the very first human beings as well. The hoofed migrants include springbok, gemsbok, kudu, and the big, placid eland, a now endangered creature that was once the mainstay of the Bushmen. Other migrating grass-eaters and browsers include water buffalo and zebra. Stalking the flanks of those migrating herds lurk the inevitable predators, including cheetahs, African hunting dogs, hyenas, and even the tough, adaptable Kalahari lion, a golden, desert-adapted subspecies. The lions can go weeks without a drink of water because they get the moisture they need from the flesh and blood of their prey.

Many of these animals move with the seasons. They cross the desert and grassland to arrive in the northern reaches near the Okavango River when water comes cascading down from the highlands to the north. The seasonal floods filter out into a marshy delta. The marsh glimmers with fish, shrimp, and insects, which attracts birds from vast distances. The crocodiles and hippopotamus who have waited out the dry season in small, permanent water sources expand out into the seasonal marshes to eat their fill. The buffalo, elephants, springboks, wildebeests, and zebras graze on the sudden flourishing of grasses, keeping a wary eye out for the lions, cheetahs, hyenas—and the occasional surviving human hunter. Ironically, tourism and the scope of long-lens cameras seem to be drawing more humans these days than the old, subsistence hunting of the Bushmen.

Still, the Kalahari remains an invaluable place to gain insight into human evolution and our impact on the environment. For instance, one recent study found evidence of a 40,000-year-old trade network in Africa, which suggests that the ancestors of the Bushmen came here in the first days of the rise of complex human societies. Researchers found some of the earliest stone tools ever documented plus tiny beads made of ostrich eggshells in the Central Rift Valley of Kenya, according to University of Illinois archaeologist Stanley Ambrose. The stone tools may date back 50,000 years, close to the time that the first human beings reached Australia, near when the Bushmen settled into the Kalahari, and perhaps as few as 20,000 years after modern humans begin moving north out of Africa.

But perhaps the most intriguing finding was the beads, which Ambrose suggests ancient artisans made to trade with other groups. Such a trade network suggests a complex, cooperative culture and economy more than 30,000 years before the first signs of agriculture. Ambrose argues that the beads suggest first a culture sufficiently complex to care about a useless item used purely for ornamentation. Moreover, the possibility of trade networks to exchange the beads indicates that people had begun to develop relationships and interconnections. Other work done with shell beads used in later trade networks suggest that a band of hunter-gatherers might shift camps hundreds of miles in a single year. That contrasts to the evidence suggesting a much simpler culture among competing groups like the *Neanderthals* in Europe, who appear to have died out shortly after modern *Homo sapiens* arrived in their planet-girdling migration out of Africa.

"The ancient beads may thus symbolize a mechanism for increased social solidarity and adaptations to risky environments. They may be a symbolic currency for exchange and obligations that can be saved for times of need, like money in the bank. People who have this social security system would compete better with others, the Neanderthals, for example, who didn't. So this improved system of regional networks and social solidarity may have allowed modern humans, when they left Africa, to out-compete and replace the Neanderthals," Ambrose concluded.

So while the Kalahari Desert seems harsh and the Bushmen who know it best seem impoverished, all *Homo sapiens* may owe a huge debt to both the hunter-gather cultures that spawned all modern civilizations and to the environmental challenges of places like the Kalahari that honed their skills and forced their innovations.

Australian Deserts

Australia

The hard, sprawling deserts of Australia and the remarkable people who have lived in them for 50,000 years offer fascinating clues to human evolution, climate shifts, and the intricate connections between living things and the *ecosystems* they inhabit (an example is shown in the color insert on page C-8). Although Australia boasts tropical forests along great sections of coast, much of the interior is divided into three great deserts, the 317,800-square-mile (823,000 sq km) Great Sandy, the 164,000-square-mile (424,400 sq km) Great Victoria, and the 56,000-square-mile (145,000 sq km) Simpson.

These mostly flat, sandy, scrubby deserts occupy most of the interior of this island continent and are sustained by the same atmospheric circulation patterns that created the deserts of the Northern Hemisphere like the Sahara. However, the vagaries of the southern oceans and the shifting monsoons make conditions in Australia less harsh and the temperatures less extreme than in the great waste of the Sahara. Moreover, Australia's long isolation from any other landmass has ensured that its plants, animals, and human cultures have evolved along distinctive and unexpected paths, creating a biological cast of characters found nowhere else.

The isolated island-continent of Australia has long provided a bizarre proving ground for theories of evolution and ecology. Some 200 million years ago, all the present-day continents were gathered into a single landmass called Pangaea. Convection currents deep within the molten Earth caused this continent to split apart and set the continents adrift, embedded on crustal plates. As the dinosaurs peaked in the Jurassic period, Australia was an island drifting out to sea, cut off from most of the plants and animals on the other continents. As a result, Australia developed a unique set of creatures. In particular, Australia remained the land of the *marsupials*, mammal-like creatures including kangaroos, wombats, bush-babies, and others whose young are born as tiny, squirmy, utterly helpless near-embryos who mature while attached to a mother's nipple tucked safely inside a protective pouch. Although such marsupials once lived all over the world, outside of Australia they generally could not compete with placental mammals, which kept their young inside the womb until they are much more developed. Only a few oddball marsupials like the opossum survived outside of Australia.

Human beings are relative newcomers to this complex web of living things. Several varieties of relatively big-brain, upright-walking, big-bodied primates with opposable thumbs spread throughout the world in the roughly 5 to 8 million years after their line diverged from their nearest primate relatives, like the chimpanzees and gorillas. Once, paleontologists thought these scattered *hominids* were the ancestors of modern humans. But more recent analysis of the DNA shared by all living human beings suggests that modern *Homo sapiens* spread out of southern Africa between 70,000 and 180,000 years ago. Perhaps as these tool-using early humans spread they drove into extinction other upright-walking primates competing for the same food resources. In any case, the first humans walked out of Africa, perhaps following the great game herds, and spread across Asia and then across ice age land bridges into North and South America.

Some 50,000 years ago, these early humans somehow crossed the open ocean to reach the shores of Australia. No one knows how they managed such a feat, but they must have fashioned rafts or dugout canoes and made their way from island to island until they reached this strange land.

Of course, like most aspects of human evolution, the details of that migration and the impact the newly arrived hunters and gatherers had on the remarkable, isolated creatures of Australia remain deeply controversial. But timing, as they say, is everything.

For instance, fossil experts quickly concluded that the arrival of the first human beings in Australia coincided with the disappearance of most

DISASTROUS EXPLORATIONS

Ironically, although the aboriginals could not withstand the Europeans in safe territory, the Europeans could barely survive in areas the aboriginals considered home. Australian history is filled with tales of disastrous attempts to explore the interior. The most renowned of the Australian explorers was Ernest Giles, who led three major expeditions to explore these great inland deserts. He named the Gibson Desert after his friend Alfred Gibson. In the midst of a trek through that desert, Gibson grew weary and ill and pleaded with Giles to turn back. Instead, Giles gave Gibson the bulk of their supplies and water and told him to backtrack to civilization. After many harrowing adventures, Giles returned safely, only to discover Gibson had disappeared into the desert. Giles, an Olympic gold medalist, nearly died of starvation and thirst due to his efforts to explore the continent's interior. Despite his courage, daring, and success, he was largely forgotten and died of pneumonia, an impoverished and unknown clerk.

of the continent's strange megafauna. Roughly 85 percent of the Australian animals weighing more than 100 (45.4 kg) pounds disappeared at this time, including 19 marsupials weighing over 220 pounds (99.8 kg). That included bizarre animals like a wombat the size of a hippopotamus, a 25-foot-long (7.62 m) snake, a 25-foot-long lizard, and a horned tortoise the size of a car.

Scientists have debated for years whether the newly arrived human beings hunted down the giant marsupials, whose great size was no protection from these top-of-the-food-chain predators. On the other hand, perhaps human beings introduced other changes into the environment that doomed the larger animals, like the early human practice of setting fire to grasslands. Or perhaps humans just happened to arrive at the same time that overall climate changes doomed many of the existing species.

Scientists have tried to solve the riddle to better understand how human beings both cause the changes that produce deserts and then survive the harsh demands of the changed conditions. But answering the many questions about this mass extinction first required a better grasp of the timing of both the arrival of the first human beings and the crash of the big marsupials.

At one time, fossil experts argued that the first humans reached Australia about 62,000 years ago. That early date was based on a complex method for dating the fossilized remains of Mungo Man and Mungo Lady, the fragmentary bones of two people who died on the shores of long-vanished Lake Mungo. At that time, an ice age gripped the planet, creating a great chain of freshwater lakes in areas long since turned to desert (which can be seen in the color insert on page C-8). The original 62,000-year-old date for those fossils stirred a hornet's buzz of debate. It placed the first humans squarely on the scene of the extinction of the continent's large marsupials. It also created great difficulties for the DNA experts who argued that modern human beings didn't start their spread out of Africa until about 80,000 years ago. It did not seem possible for humans to have so quickly spread all the way from Africa into Asia and hop islands across the Indian Ocean to Australia.

However, after years of debate, scientists now mostly agree that Mungo Man lived only about 40,000 years ago, which is more consistent with other studies that date the oldest stone tools found so far in Australia back to about 50,000 years, according to a study published in the journal *Nature*. The firm dating of Mungo Man in the midst of the last ice age now makes it possible to study the way in which early human beings responded to dramatic and relentless changes forced by a shift in climate, which converted much of Australia from a wet, lake-speckled mosaic of grasslands and woodlands into an unrelenting desert.

Much of the evidence suggests that human beings sometimes adapted to those changes and sometimes forced changes of their own. One fascinating attempt to measure the impact of human beings depended on a careful analysis of the fossil eggshells of several giant, ostrichlike birds, the emu and the extinct genyornis, according to an article published in the journal *Science*.

The scientists used certain elements in eggshell fragments dating back some 65,000 years to figure out what these two giant, flightless birds were eating. For instance, plants that depend on summer rains use a slightly different method of converting the Sun's rays into energy, which affects the type of carbon molecules in the plants' tissues. By contrast, plants that live in desert areas that do not get summer rains will produce a different ratio of carbon. The emus and genyornis eat grass and shrubs, which means that distinctive ratio of different isotopes of carbon are reflected in the composition of their eggshells. Therefore, by looking at the types of carbon stashed in the fossilized eggshells, scientists can tell whether those long dead emus and genyornis were eating grass and shrubs growing in a wet grassland or a dry desert.

The study yielded a fascinating glimpse of the shift from the wet ice age climate to the arid deserts of today. The scientists concluded that summer storms brought plenty of rain deep into the interior of Australia between 65,000 and 45,000 years ago, coinciding with the ice age arrival of the first human beings. But sometime between 30,000 and 15,000 years ago, everything changed. The summer rains failed, and the forests

KANGAROO HOPS HAPPILY THROUGH HARD TIMES

The kangaroo remains the most distinctive and recognizable marsupial in Australia. Although Australia separated from Antarctica and begin drifting north 64 million to 136 million years ago, the ancestors of the first, ratlike marsupials hopped out of the trees some 30 million years ago. They eventually gave rise to kangaroos and their various relatives, all called macropods. Their speed, versatility, and water-thrifty construction preadapted them to desert living. Now they range from the tiny, one-pound musky rat-kangaroo to the bounding 175-pound red kangaroo. These largest of kangaroos are especially adapted to the desert, since they get much of their necessary moisture from the food they eat. Other kangaroos live in trees while their close relatives the wallabies occupy a variety of specialized niches.

A study of the 40,000-year-old bones of kangaroos and other marsupials in Australia suggests that most species have gotten progressively smaller, perhaps reflecting the gradual shift from the grasslands and forests of the ice age climate to the deserts of today. Overall, most species are about 30 percent smaller than their ancestors of 20,000 to 40,000 years ago. Some scientists speculate that they have adapted to an increasingly arid climate. Others believe the shift reflects pressure from human hunters, who have consistently targeted the largest animals.

and grasslands changed into desert. That probably reflected climatic shifts that moved the summer monsoon storms away from Australia to now drench India. As a result, even though many areas of Australia's interior get 10 inches of rain a year, which makes them almost lush by desert standards, the long, dry, rainless summer creates a harsh environment for both plants and animals.

The sad fate of genyornis suggests that human beings may have dramatically increased the impact of the underlying shifts in climate. This speedy, 200-pound (91 kg) flightless bird lived in the vast interior of the continent until about 50,000 years ago, just when human beings arrived. The analysis of its eggshells shows that before human beings arrived, genyornis mostly ate bushes and shrubs. By contrast, the more flexible emu also ate grasses. But the eggshells show that 50,000 years ago, the grasslands expanded and the areas with shrubs dwindled sharply, leading to the extinction of the grass-shunning genyornis. So the expansion of the grassland and the extinction of many of the megafauna actually came a little ahead of the climate change.

Some experts say that means human beings must have contributed to the extinction of the genyornis and many other species. Gifford Miller, a geochronologist at the University of Colorado at Boulder, suspects that the newly arrived human beings started deliberately setting fire to the grasslands, which was a common practice among Native Americans as well. These hunters and gatherers observed that fires usually stimulate the spread of grasslands, which yield many foods and support key species they liked to hunt. Miller's analysis of the eggshells and climates shifts suggest that the effect of the newly arrived human hunters was heightened by their tendency to set fires to expand grasslands, which then became deserts as the climate shifted.

However, other scientists continue to debate the impact of humans. One study published recently in the *Proceedings of the National Academy of Sciences* concluded that many large creatures like a 6,000-pound (2,722 kg) wombat, a fierce marsupial "lion," and the biggest lizard in history did not die out until 30,000 years ago, which means they probably coexisted with human beings for at least 15,000 years. That would mean the shift in the summer monsoon patterns did more to cause their extinction than the arrival of human beings. These findings were based on a new method of measuring rare earth elements absorbed by fossil bones from the soil in which they are embedded, which supported a much younger age for certain key fossils than earlier methods.

Of course, more recent, drastic ecological changes are theoretically easier to document than ancient shifts. For instance, a study of 300-year-old emu eggs documented another shift from grasslands toward desert that took place when the first Europeans brought sheep and cattle to the continent. Once again, the scientists used radio carbon dating to figure out how old the eggshells were, then analyzed the carbon in the *amino acids* in the shells to figure out what the birds were eating. The study demonstrated that the introduction of domestic livestock resulted in a sharp drop in the total biomass of plants. Essentially, emus had to give up eating grass entirely, since the cows and sheep gobbled the surviving grasses down to the nub.

Those studies document the dramatic transformation of a grassland into a harsh desert, shoved along first by the introduction of fire by the first humans and then by livestock brought in by the second wave of immigrants.

THE ABORIGINALS: THE OLDEST CULTURE

The Australian deserts also harbor one of the most remarkable, desert-adapted cultures, the Australian aboriginals. They adapted to the harsh conditions and their long isolation with a culture sparing in the use of tools but rich in philosophy and cultural adjustments to desert conditions. Moreover, their long isolation from other human cultures has made them a key piece in the attempt to reconstruct the puzzle of human evolution and adaptation.

No one knows how the first people made it to Australia perhaps 50,000 years ago. They may have been fishermen on rafts or dugouts who made the journey across open water, island hopping from Asia through the scatter of islands that constitute Indonesia and finally happening upon Australia. That implies a relatively sophisticated and adventurous human culture capable of undertaking such a journey 50,000 years ago.

Numerous studies of these isolated people have attempted to shed light on the still-emerging theories of human evolution and spread. The DNA-based evidence of a recent spread of modern humans out of Africa makes the original inhabitants of Australia a crucial link in the chain of human evolution, since they made their way to the island continent soon after people first spread out of Africa and then remained genetically isolated for 50,000 years.

One recent study that relied heavily on comparing the DNA of Australian aboriginals to other groups concluded that modern humans first left Africa just 70,000 years ago, at which time their world population totaled maybe 2,000, according to a recent study by researchers from Stanford University published in the *American Journal of Human Genetics*. That could account for the tiny genetic difference between modern human populations, much smaller than the genetic differences between different groups of chimpanzees, gorillas, or most other animals.

The people who did reach Australia 50,000 to 60,000 years ago initially found a much more lush place, fragrant with grasslands, flowers, and strange animals. But when the climate changed and huge areas of the island continent shifted to desert between 5,000 and 10,000 years ago, the aboriginals demonstrated the great secret survival weapon of human beings—adaptability.

The native people of Australia developed a rich weaving of cultures. Many groups invented their own languages. By the time Europeans arrived in the 1800s, the scattered groups of hunters and gatherers spoke at least 500 languages in 31 different language groups. Often, people living on one side of a rich area like Sydney Bay would speak a completely different language from the people on the other side of the bay. Most of the estimated 300,000 native people living in Australia before the arrival of the first Europeans lived along the fertile, well-watered coast. But many also made a living in the harsh interior.

They made use of every resource, including insects. For instance, they staged feasts and ceremonials to gather up the Bogong moth, which congregated in mountain caves each year. During the moth season, people would go to the mountains, enter the moth caves, and gather up a great feast. They could stir the moths into hot sand and ashes to singe off the wings and legs, before using a net to sift out the heads and bodies. They then ate the cooked bodies of the moths like popcorn or ground them into a paste. The moths proved an excellent food source, with an average fat content of about 50 percent.

Another great delicacy was the witchety grub, found on the roots of witchety bushes in central Australia. These grubs were among the most important foods for desert-dwelling aboriginals. People would dig up the roots and split them open to extract the grub within. Popped into the ashes, the grubs would swell up and stiffen. They taste like almonds and are so rich in calories, protein, and fat that 10 grubs a day provided enough calories to sustain a human being. Other insect foods included the honeypot ants, which serve as living storage containers for nectar collected by worker ants. The native people also treasured the stored honey of the native, stingless bees. They would catch a bee feeding on pollen then glue a little bit of wood to the bee's feet. This would slow the bee enough on its trip back to the hive that the hunter could follow the bee and harvest the stored honey.

LIVING IN DREAMTIME

Perhaps the most remarkable adaptation of these desert-dwelling people was their rich, mystical culture, layered with stories and stitched together with faith and insight into the natural world. The Australian aboriginals boast the longest continuous cultural history of any group on Earth. Central to their view of the world is the mysterious and transcendent notion of dreamtime, a belief that explains how the universe came to be, the creation of human beings, and the purpose of creation. This philosophy held that all living things are part of a vast network of relationships connected to the spirits that created the Earth and the dream that contains it. The aboriginals believe that every event leaves a record in the land, so that every place, animal, plant, and person has some connection to those original stories and spirits, which makes everything sacred. Dreamtime existed before the Earth and so brought it into being. Now, dreamtime continues as an echo or shadow of the Earth, which means it remains accessible to a reverent and respectful person. Dreams provide one of the best connections to this underlying spiritual reality.

The desert-dwelling aboriginals speak of *jiva* or *guruwari*, a seed power deposited in the earth. Every activity and life leaves what amounts to a vibration, just as plants leave a copy of themselves in the enigmatic form of a seed. The mountains, rocks, riverbeds, and waterholes all create their own vibration in dreamtime and so remain connected to the origins of the Earth and the spirits that still animate it. So in this concept, the world is merely an expression of a deeper underlying reality, which people can glimpse only in certain states of spirituality or consciousness or dreams.

The complex skein of stories passed along for the past 50,000 years connect certain places with events in that dreamtime of creation and to plants and animals and their animating spirit. Therefore the stories and ceremonies connect the ethics and the morality of people directly to the landscape in which they live. At the same time, those stories all incorporate rocks, mountains, rivers, streambeds, and other features of the landscape. That means that people who learn the stories of dreamtime and the creation myths will in that process memorize a map of their territory, which will help them find food, water, seasonal resources, and territories of other bands. So as a hunter walks along he will see a certain outcropping and remember the story of where the echidna-spirit slept for three years and from that story will know he will find a reliable spring a mile to the southwest.

Interestingly, these beliefs echo the philosophy and spirituality of desert-dwelling tribes on the other side of the world, including the Chemehuevi Indians of California and the Tohono O'odham and the Apache in Arizona. All have developed traditional beliefs that imbued the landscape and all living creatures with elements of the sacred, urged people to live good lives, and used stories about certain places to teach right behavior and philosophy. Interestingly, most of the world's great religions originated in desert cultures, which perhaps reflects the austere and mystical impact of living in such a sparse, difficult landscape, where people must rely on a unreliable bounty of rainfall or irregular blooms of crucial plants.

Those aboriginal beliefs help account for the extraordinary reverence the native people feel for Uluru, perhaps the world's largest rock, a mass of sandstone 1,100 feet high (335.3 m), two miles long (3.22 km), and half a mile (0.80 km) wide that rises from the deserts of north-central Australia, one of the most stirring sights on the planet because of its sheer size and graceful, irresistible curves. The creation stories of the Anangu and others revolve around the massive sandstone formation. One dome-shaped stone is said to be one of the digging sticks of the ancients. Another story holds that gouges in the rock are the scars of the spears of the creators.

The ancient culture of the aboriginals was decimated soon after the first Europeans came upon Australia, starting in 1788. The British originally used the continent as a prison for criminals transported there for crimes committed in England. But the introduction of new people, plants, animals, and diseases laid waste to the aboriginal cultures. Within a century, the aboriginal population had dropped by 90 percent. Many of the surviving native people retreated into the interior, which remained too harsh for the Europeans to claim.

9

Gobi Desert
Central Asia

The dry, wind-tormented sands of the 500,000-square-mile (1.3 million sq km) Gobi Desert harbor deep secrets—from the evolution of life to the restless stirrings of the planet. The high, windy, bone-dry region is a continental desert as a result of the mountains that surround it and cut it off from moist, ocean air in the middle of the Eurasian continent. The titanic surrounding mountain systems wring all the moisture out of the air before it reaches the Gobi, creating one of the world's largest desert regions.

The arid conditions that have stripped the Gobi of soil and stunted its plants and animals have also made it one of the great research laboratories for scientists studying climate and prehistoric life. The massive, unstable sand dunes of the Gobi have persisted for millions of years. Abrupt sand slides rushing down the slope of dunes hundreds of feet high some 80 million years ago buried dinosaurs and other creatures alive and in recent years have yielded some of the world's best-preserved fossils. These fossils have transformed our understanding of dinosaurs, illuminated the links between dinosaurs and birds, and even revealed telling details about our own mammalian ancestry. Moreover, the hardships of the desert and the grasslands that surround it spawned the nomadic Mongol cultures, which at one point under the leadership of brilliant and ruthless leaders like Genghis Khan ruled much of the known world.

The great bulk of the Gobi is a vast plain with soils made of chalks and limestone sediments laid down in the Cenozoic era (up to 66 million years ago). High, cold, nearly waterless, and far from the moderating effects of the ocean, the Gobi is a land of extremes. Lows in January in many areas plunge to –40°F (4°C), while summer highs can soar to 113°F (45°C).

ASSEMBLING A CONTINENTAL DESERT

Almost unimaginable forces raised the vast network of surrounding mountain ranges that created the Gobi Desert. Understanding the

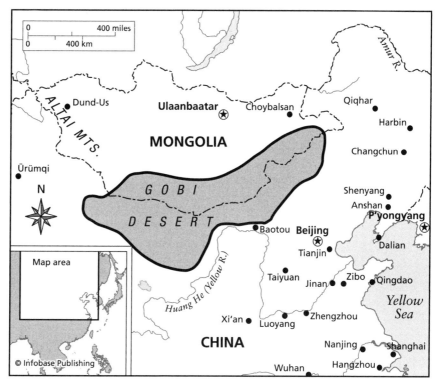

Gobi Desert

creation of the Gobi requires an understanding of plate tectonics and the theory of *continental drift*. Geologists have discovered that the Earth's surface is divided into a series of crustal plates that include both heavier oceanic material and lighter continental material. These cooler and more solid surface parts of the Earth's rock crust move slowly over time across the hotter, weaker, underlying asthenosphere atop Earth's semimolten mantle. The mantle churns with great convection currents that well up against the bottom of this thin, cool, brittle layer of crustal rock. Those currents cause great cracks to form in the oceanic crust along the deep ocean ridges and trenches. Molten magma pushing up from the mantle constantly adds new rock to the oceanic plate margins, and the lighter rocks comprising the continents go along for the ride.

The story of the Gobi Desert really started 100 million years ago when movements of crustal plates began to assemble modern Asia. At that time, India was an island continent, much like present-day Australia. Previously, it had been part of a single, great supercontinent scientists have named Gondwanaland. The fragmented pieces of this supercontinent broke up and began to drift with the movements of the oceanic plates. At some point, as a result of still poorly understood changes deep in the Earth, the mass of light crustal rock that makes up India spun, shifted, and headed north at what rates as breakneck speed in geology. No one knows for sure why this rogue continent started scooting along three or four times as fast as any crustal plates are moving today. The leading theory suggests that the plate was being pulled from the north, where it was plunging in under the edge of Asia at the same time it was being

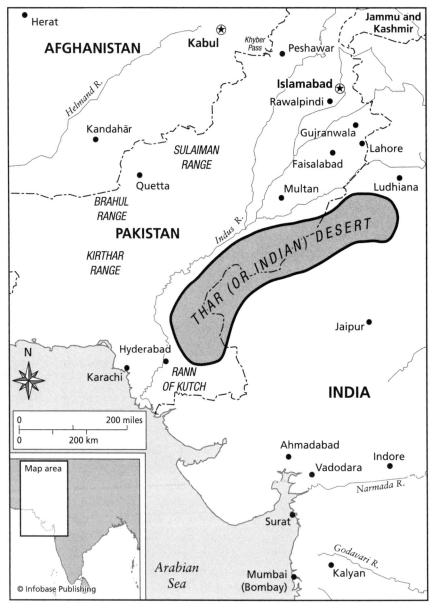

Thar Desert

pushed from the south by vigorous seafloor spreading along a mid-ocean ridge. Light continental rock usually does not get caught under the edge of a plate of dense, heavy seafloor rock. So once the leading edge of the plate got subducted under the edge of another plate, the heavy overlying rock drove it down quickly. Moreover, the plate might have split over a hot spot in the mantle where the deep currents drove superheated rock against the crust. As a result, the combined pull from the north and push from the south created a great, continental pileup.

This caused perhaps the most titanic geologic collision in history. Some 55 million years ago, India plowed into Asia. The edges of both continents were made of light rock, so instead of one going down under the other, they created a massive pileup. This created the Tibetan Plateau, an immense upland that forms the highest region on the planet, with an average elevation of 15,000 feet (5,000 m). It includes most of the world's highest mountains, including Mount Everest in the Himalayas. The Earth's crust is thicker here than anywhere else.

CUTTING OFF THE MOISTURE

The collision of continents ultimately isolated the portion of central Asia that includes the Gobi Desert from the moisture-laden winds from the ocean. The winds blowing up against this barrier of mountains rose until the moisture it contained condensed into rain or froze into snow. The

---

PLATE TECTONICS: THE RESTLESS EARTH

The Earth's surface is divided into several major crustal plates, layers of light rock 30 to 100 miles (48–160 km) thick floating on top of the Earth's heavy, iron-rich mantle. Currents that originate in the molten, super-dense core trigger inexorable currents in the mantle above. The currents in the mantle, in turn, push up against the light, brittle rock of the crust. Those forces create cracks in the crust that can run for thousands of miles. Where the mantle current wells up against the underside of the crust it creates a crack through which molten rock oozes from below. When the magma reaches the surface, it builds great chains of volcanoes and mountain ranges like the Mid-Atlantic Ridge, which runs down the middle of the Atlantic Ocean. Here, the extrusion of new molten oceanic crust from below forces two crustal plates apart. At the opposite side of such a crustal plate, those same mantle currents can shove light crustal rock back down into the Earth. Here, a five- to seven-mile-deep undersea trench forms. So the rock of the Earth's oceanic crust is continually created at one edge of a crustal plate and destroyed at the other edge. This system of plate tectonics dominates the surface of the Earth and controls the destiny of all living things.

The even lighter rocks of the Earth's continents "float" on top of the oceanic crust. That means the continents are like rafts, carried along on the conveyor belt of the moving crustal plates in which they are embedded. The collision of continents and crustal plates largely determine the distribution of the world's deserts.

Gobi sits surrounded by such a ring of mountains, including the Tibetan plateau to the southwest, the Altai Mountains and grassland steppes of Mongolia on the north, and the vast north China plain to the southwest. Gobi means "desert" in Mongolian, but is also known in Chinese as the *sha-mo* (sand desert) and *han-hal* (dry sea). It encompasses several adjacent dry basins, although some geographers divide them into separate deserts.

A high desert far from the moderating influence of the oceans, the Gobi's climate is one of great extremes, including rapid changes in temperature and furious windstorms. This high, arid region is divided into different areas: the Ka-Shun, Dzungarian, and Trans-Altai Gobi in the west, the Mongolian Gobi in the middle and east, and finally the Ala Shan Desert in the south.

Most of those regions are nearly barren. The Ka-Shun rises to some 5,000 feet (1,700 m), with long, corrugations of 300-foot-tall (91.44 m) hills, hollows, and jagged crests. The region gets only a few inches of rain a year and supports few plants, animals, streams, or springs. In low-lying depressions, water intermittently collects to support salt marshes, where only plants adapted to high concentrations of salts and other minerals in the soil can survive. The Trans Altai Gobi is a high, rugged plain bounded by mountain ranges, separated by ravines and extensive salt marshes, where the four inches (100 mm) of rain annually support only scattered plants and animals. The Ka-Shun Gobi, lying between the China-Mongolia border and the Yellow River, is a vast plain covered with sand.

EASTERN GOBI DESERT STEPPE

The region most typically desert is the Eastern Gobi desert steppe, which covers some 109,000 square miles (281,800 sq km) and extends from the Inner Mongolian plateau in China north into Mongolia. High and cold with elevations from 2,300 to 5,000 feet (770–1,700 m), this region gets as much as eight inches (200 mm) of rain a year, roughly twice the rainfall of other portions of the Gobi. Although that is not enough rain to sustain actual surface rivers, underground rivers do flow through the porous sands and great basins. These rivers feed springs and wells, which makes this region much easier to settle than the rest of the Gobi. To the north, the Eastern Gobi gives way to the high grasslands that spawned the Mongols and the world-conquering Genghis Khan. The Eastern Gobi consists of broad flat basins separated by low mountain ranges, broad tablelands, and flat plains. Some of the low, stretched, and slumping basins between the worn and weary mountains sometimes catch enough runoff to create lakes, often heavy with salt and dissolved minerals from the millions of years of runoff and evaporation.

ALSHAN PLATEAU AND JUNGGAR BASIN SEMI-DESERTS

Two major areas adjacent to the deep desert, the Alshan Plateau and the Junggar Basin, transition from barren sand to arid grasslands. The Little Gobi desert lies in the southwestern portion of the larger desert area. Higher and wetter, it fills the space between the Yellow River on the east and a mountain chain. It lies in one of the three great depressions caused by the stretching and lifting caused by the collision of continents. An inland sea probably filled this vast basin during the wet ice ages, but now it is filled with layers of clay and sand. The seemingly lifeless sand flats cover hundreds of square miles, utterly waterless with scarcely an oasis or a hint of green.

Only a handful of plants can grow in such harsh conditions, including a few types of bushes and a dozen grasses and herbs. A few other creatures eke out a living from those scattered grasses and shrubs, including antelopes, wolves, foxes, hares, hedgehogs, many lizards, and a few birds.

Caught between two long ridges, the Junggar Basin is marked by a great swelling in the crust of Earth between the ridges. The small Ghashiun-Gobi salt desert is barren and lifeless. It seems made of broken remnants of the Earth, eroded mountains, sandy flats, salt soiled depressions, and shattered rock. Only a few hares, antelopes, and wild camels can survive, moving great distances to reach the limited areas with grass and shrubs.

SAND AND SOIL

Sand defines the Gobi Desert, the dried-out remains of soils that once sustained life during the ice ages. Unlike soil, sand lacks the organic material to nurture plant life. Experts still puzzle over the source of the great, hypnotic fields of massive sand dunes that dominate hundreds of square miles of the nearly rainless desert. Some insist that the sand dunes are fed by sediments deposited thousands of years ago in great lakes that

WILDLIFE OF THE GOBI DESERT

The harsh conditions of the Gobi have forced the creatures that live there to adapt and survive. Although much of the desert consists of sandy or stony plains, the mountains, canyons, springs, marshes, and fitful river systems provide enough diversity of habitat to shelter an array of fascinating creatures. These include wild Bactrian camels, several species of bears, argali sheep, Siberian ibex, hulan or the Asiatic wild ass, wolves, black vultures, Asiatic long-eared hedgehogs, black-tailed and Mongolian antelope, and even the snow leopard in mountain ranges in and near the Gobi.

accumulated in the great basins and depressions that became the Gobi Desert. They maintain that the sand came from soil washed out of the nearby mountains plus the limestone skeletons of microscopic creatures that lived in those ancient inland seas.

However, other experts have found evidence that the great, planetary wind patterns blew much of the sand and soil into the enclosed basins from across much of Asia. They point to the worn, blasted chains of hills and mountains that lie scattered throughout the uplands and tablelands of the Gobi plus the great windstorms that blow across northern China and the Russian steppes and into the region. Viewed from space, the desert's great chains of sand dunes align with prevailing wind patterns and the great, seasonal shifts in wind directions. Measurements of individual sand dunes in wind-plagued areas like Takla Makan have recorded movements of as much as 150 feet (50 m) in a single year.

The dust-covered plains of the Gobi and northern China constitute one of the planet's greatest expanses of *loess*, which is made of fine dust transported long distances by the wind. In the Gobi, the loess layers are 30 or 40 feet (10–12 m) thick, deposited by the wind and composed of a fine dust of limestone made from the skeletons of sea creatures. Most of the layer formed during the ice ages, after the inexorable movement of glaciers ground limestone layers into fine powder. When the glaciers retreated and released the pulverized limestone soil, the fierce winds picked it up and blew it into the Gobi. Here, it formed layers of sandstone soft enough for the people living in the area to dig cavelike houses out of the cliffs and hills.

The fine, dry soils of the Gobi still affect the rest of the planet. For instance, one recent study tracked a dust storm in the Gobi Desert that grew so fierce that it rose high into the atmosphere. There, high-altitude wind currents dispersed the dust throughout the world. All across Asia, airports shut down for lack of visibility. Studies show that the distinctive limestone dust of the Gobi can cross the ocean and waft to Earth in the United States and elsewhere.

SAND DUNES SWALLOW DINOSAURS

Despite the scale of the great Gobi sand dunes, it is still startling to learn that more than 65 million years ago those sand dunes were big enough to bury a dinosaur in an instant. At least, that is the conclusion of an international team of scientists who published a study in *Geology*.

The Gobi Desert has long been renowned as a fossil hunter's dream. Roy Andrews Chapman, a swashbuckling, publicity-grabbing scientist who became the model for the Indiana Jones movies, first discovered the surprisingly well-preserved dinosaur bones and eggs in the dry sands of the Gobi. Scientists have been mounting expeditions to that remote region ever since, trying to piece together a history of the dinosaurs.

A team of scientists writing in *Geology* has suggested a fascinating theory to explain the extraordinary preservation of dinosaur bones in the Gobi. Working in the Ukhaa Tolgod (brown hills), they sought an explanation for the rich variety of perfectly preserved fossils. They found they could study tiny skeletal structures in the buried bones, including features smaller than one of the letters in this sentence. Scientists have found the remains of fierce meat-eaters larger than tyrannosaurus rex, perfectly preserved with scarcely a bone missing. They sought to explain how an entire dinosaur was killed and buried so quickly that not even the quickest scavengers or bone-eating bacteria could get to the remains before the fossilization process started.

The scientists proposed a massive sand slide—an avalanche of water-saturated sand down the steeply curving side of a sand dune tall enough to dwarf even a 52-foot-long (14 m) monster like the tarbosaurus, a close relative of the tyrannosaurus. The geologists found three different types of sandstone at the site.

THE FIRST INDIANA JONES

Roy Chapman Andrews had a very odd dream for a young boy roaming the hills of Wisconsin. He wanted to work for the American Museum of Natural History in New York City. But his life exceeded even his wildest dreams and included dinosaurs, bandits, international fame, and a career so exciting he became the model for the swashbuckling *archaeologist* of the Indiana Jones movies.

The minute Andrews graduated from college in 1906, he headed for New York and offered to sweep the museum's floors. Instead, the director gave him a job mixing clay and setting up the dramatic exhibits of elephants, lions, and other creatures stuffed and frozen into fierce postures. One thing led to another and soon the young, audacious Andrews was leading museum expeditions. He explored the forests of Korea and chased whales in the Pacific. He learned so much about whales that the museum asked him to help design and set up the internationally renowned blue whale skeleton that now hangs in the entry of the museum.

But he gained his greatest fame with a series of five expeditions he led into the Gobi Desert looking for dinosaur fossils. The major 1925 expedition included 40 men, eight cars, and 75 camels, used to stash food and fuel along the route. Andrews had to contend with heat, howling desert windstorms, and the constant threat of bandits. The dashing Andrews said of the bandits "they swarm like devouring locusts."

His expeditions gained international acclaim and focused international attention on dinosaurs. He claimed to have found the first dinosaur eggs, although a French team later disputed his contention. He also found perfectly preserved in the desert sands the bones of the Baluchitherium, then thought to be the largest land mammal ever. He eventually became director of the museum he had volunteered to sweep. After a long and colorful career that made science an adventure for the public, he retired to write books, including *In the Day of the Dinosaur*, published in 1959, the year before he died.

One had clearly visible layers tilted at a 25-degree angle and sorted by particle size, exactly the sort of sandstone that forms when a sand dune gets buried, compressed, and converted into rock. Some researchers had long ago suggested that the sandstorms creating such massive sand dunes might have suffocated and buried the dinosaurs, which would account for the well-preserved remains. Surprisingly, the researchers found very few fossils in these sand-dune-created sandstones.

The second type of sandstone had a different structure, but had clearly originally been laid down by the wind. The paleontologists found burrow marks made by insects and other small creatures that had dug into the surface of the dunes, but only below a certain depth. They concluded that this sandstone represented a flat, wind-blown layer and that dinosaurs had ambled over the surface and therefore crushed the insect and animal burrows in the upper levels, leaving the lower ones intact. This layer representing the windblown surface of a sand dune also contained no dinosaur fossils.

Almost all of the dinosaur fossils were found in the third type. This layer of sandstone proved much more surprising. The rock showed no structure or layering, as it would if laid down on top of a sand dune or in a bottomland deposit between dunes. Moreover, this type of sandstone contained rocks and pebbles much too large to be carried by the wind. Clearly, the dinosaurs buried and fossilized in this rock layer were not smothered by the sand-thick wind and then buried by the windblown sand. But scientists initially could not figure out how such a jumbled up layer of sand wound up with all of the fossils.

Fortunately, University of Nebraska geosciences professor David Loope had previously studied the Nebraska sandhills, much smaller dunes in a much wetter climate. He had collected strange stories of dunes that had suddenly collapsed and buried pickup trucks and other objects. In one case, a rain-drenched dune slid down and swallowed up most of a barn. Clearly, the wet, heavy sand dunes were prone to massive avalanches of sand. Loope concluded that in the Gobi's much wetter climate some 70 million years ago, the gigantic dunes became water-saturated in a storm and so slid down to bury an unsuspecting dinosaur at the base of the dune. That means that the dunes of the dinosaurs were probably wet, covered with vegetation, and not moving about constantly with the wind. They would have contained more clay, which would hold water until it got wet and slippery, at which point the clay layers would promote a catastrophic collapse. The overlying sand then protected the bones of the buried dinosaurs from scavengers, and the lack of oxygen deep beneath the sand prevented bacteria from breaking down the bones. As a result, the skeleton remained intact long enough for dissolved minerals in groundwater to crystallize and replace the organic material.

Various expeditions have uncovered remarkable dramas. One expedition located the nearly complete skeletons of two tarbosaurus, the largest known dinosaur predator. One had unlaid eggs still in her body. The sand preserved the details so perfectly that paleontologists could even study the barely formed bones of the embryos inside the eggs. Another expedition found the bones of a meat-eating dinosaur and his plant-eating victim entangled in the midst of their fatal struggle at the moment the avalanche of sand overwhelmed them both.

That remarkable preservation has yielded repeated surprises and inspired many scientific expeditions to the Gobi. For instance, one expedition found the oldest marsupial. Another expedition to the same area as the sand slide study discovered the well-preserved, 80-million-year-old bones of a tiny creature that lived in the dark shadow of the dinosaurs. The opossumlike delatheridium had sharp molars and long canines and a two-inch-long skull. It probably ate lizards and other early mammals. Scientists were surprised to find that creature in the Gobi Desert, since the marsupials today live mostly in South America and Australia. This finding suggests that the marsupial line originated in Asia and spread across the planet, but then died out in Asia in the face of competition from the placental mammals.

THE FIRST BIRD

Another fossil from the same area revealed new insights into how birds developed the ability to fly, according to findings in *Science*. The fossilized bones and feather impressions of the pigeon-sized bird dubbed *Apsaravis ukhaana* were uncovered in Ukhaa Tolgod in the Gobi. The creature appears to be very close to the root of the family tree of birds, which means that virtually all birds alive today may have descended from this humble beginning and that the first birds coexisted for a time with the last of the dinosaurs. The discovery rebutted the previous theory that the first birds evolved near the seashore. Previously, the fossil evidence suggested that at this time two major lines of birds existed, but that all of the species living away from the seashore died out 65 million years ago along with the dinosaurs. This latest fossil demonstrated that this ancestor bird living far from shore among the then-damp dunes of the Gobi not only outlived the dinosaurs but left descendants who proliferated into all the bird species known today. But despite its feathers and wings, an avalanche of sand caught it along with the great dinosaurs that were doomed to extinction. Perhaps this ancient bird even made a living picking insects off the hides of giant dinosaurs, just as many birds do on elephants and hippos today.

The fossilized ancestral bird found in the Gobi also provides fascinating new insights into how birds learned to fly. The sands of the Gobi preserved the buried bird so perfectly that scientists could study the way in which a muscle attached to the bone of its wing. This muscle connection in living birds helps the bird shift from an upstroke to a downstroke, which is essential in active flying instead of passive gliding. Certain versions of this bone and muscle connection appear in *theropod dinosaurs*, but the Gobi fossil had the more advanced refinement necessary for true, powered flight. All birds today have this muscle structure, but the Gobi fossil was the oldest example of this arrangement in any fossil. The find, possible only because of the desert's ability to preserve even these ancient traces, pushes back the dawn of true, powered flight by anything besides insects to 80 million years. So the collision of continents, the rise of mountains, and the collapse of ancient wet dunes have yielded solutions to fundamental mysteries.

10

Atacama

The Oldest Desert: South America

The ancient, cold Atacama Desert might as well be on another plan-et. In fact, when scientists wanted to find a place harsh enough to test the robots they planned to send to Mars to look for the faintest, most beleaguered traces of life, they came first to this 700-mile-long (1,100 km) desert in northern Chile, where some areas go 17 years without a trace of rain.

The Atacama Desert remains the planet's oldest and driest desert, perched on a ledge of rock between the massive, jutting Andes Mountains and the 1,500-foot-high (500 m) wall of rock and cliffs that plunges into the Pacific Ocean. Just offshore lies the six-mile-deep (9.65 km) Atacama Trench, a rift along the edge of two crustal plates that helps sustain this high desert.

The Atacama Desert lies mostly between the south bend of the Loa River and the mountains that separate the Salado-Copianpo drainage ba-sins running north to the border with Peru. The desert is divided by a line of low costal mountains, which are really 5,000-foot-high (1700 m) foothills to the Andes.

The desert itself consists mostly of great flat areas covered by pebbles left behind when the wind blew away the sand and the memory of top-soil, much of it at an elevation of about 3,000 feet (1,000 m). Low-lying salt flats at the foot of the coastal mountains mark the location of lakes that dried up long ago. Small sand dunes cover less than 10 percent of the desert, as the wind continues to sort through sand delivered to this low, waterless region millions of years ago.

The coast of Chile lacks the wide, fertile coastal plain that marks most continental edges. Instead, the coastal mountains go right up to the edge of the ocean, where 1,000-foot-high (304.8 m) cliffs drop straight into the sea.

In portions of the Atacama, 16,000-foot (4,877 m) volcanic cones rise from the flat, leafless plain. These volcanoes are driven by the same

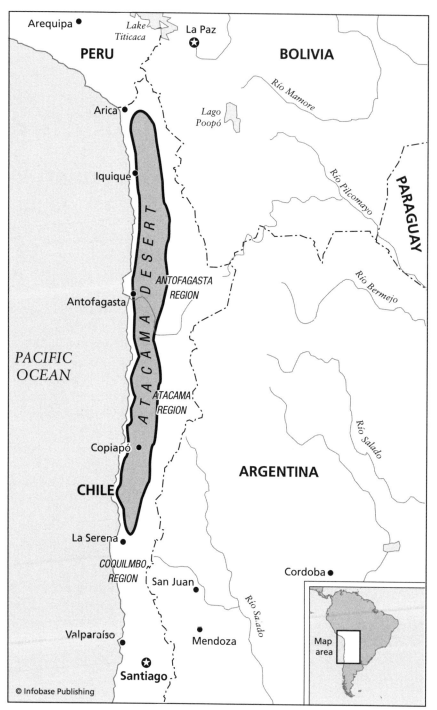

Atacama Desert

jostling of continents that continues to raise up the Andes and that dug the long, undersea trench running just offshore.

In stark contrast to the Sahara, the Atacama is a cold desert as a result of the high elevation and its position on the globe. Summer temperatures in most areas average just 66°F (19°C). The nearby ocean generates regular fog banks and cloud banks, but virtually no rain. Some areas routinely go without a trace of rain in a year and some can remain dry for decades. When storms do break through the natural barriers, they can sometimes deliver a scouring deluge. However, that happens about once every 25 to 50 years.

The Atacama has been a desert for more than 150 million years, according to recent studies. That makes it by far the oldest desert on the planet. But 150 million years is an unimaginable amount of time for a place to remain climatically stable. Remember, just 200 million years ago, all of the continents on the planet were assembled into a single supercontinent, on which the first dinosaurs roamed and roared. Back then, Africa and South America were pasted together, as were North America and Europe. So why has the Atacama remained a desert as the planet has changed around it?

Reconstructing the climate of the Atacama for the past 150 million years ago took some remarkable scientific detective work, according to a study by a team of British and South American scientists published recently in the *Journal of the Geological Society of London*. They pulled together many other studies of the mostly volcanic rocks found in that desert. When molten rocks cool, tiny magnetic minerals in the magma align with the north and south magnetic poles of the planet. Once the rock cools, those tiny, natural compasses remain locked into position, aligned on a north-south axis. If the continent on which the rocks rest moves, the magnetic particles in the rocks do not realign themselves. Moreover, periodically, the poles of the Earth flip-flop, so north becomes south. No one understands why this happens, but it is related to convection currents in the Earth's semimolten core. The core remains molten because many rocks have a natural radioactivity, so they generate a tiny amount of heat as they degrade, which increases with depth in the Earth. Given enough heat, the rocks melt. This flip-flopping of the Earth's magnetic poles is preserved in the magnetic orientation of the elements in magma and can serve as a geological clock. Therefore, geologists can use the magnetic orientation of minerals in these volcanic rocks to figure out where those rocks were sitting when they cooled and the magnetic flecks pointed north. All of that enabled geologists to pinpoint the location of the Atacama Desert throughout the past 150 million years.

In addition, geologists can figure out past climate from looking at fossils and layers of sediments in ancient lake bottoms, river courses, and

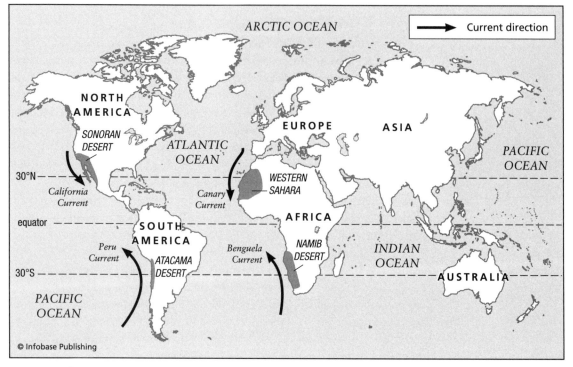

West Coast deserts

other areas. Fortunately, the geologists trying to figure out the history of the Atacama Desert had a wealth of well-dated sedimentary layers and ancient lakebeds to assemble into their geologic jigsaw puzzle.

They concluded that the chunk of South America that contains the Atacama Desert reached its present position 150 million years ago. At that point, it got caught by the Atacama Trench, which runs along the edge of a crustal plate. And when it comes to making a desert, that old real estate adage applies—location, location, location.

The Atacama developed as a desert for three main reasons. First, it sits in a spot where cold, dry air descends to the Earth's surface. The Earth's weather patterns are driven largely by the difference in temperature between the sun-drenched Tropics and the ice-shrouded poles, which is caused by the tilt of the planet. The equator is hotter because the sun's rays hit it more directly than at the poles. The heated air at the equator rises and then flows either north or south as cooler air rushes toward the equator to take its place. As the hot tropical air rises, it cools and drops its moisture on the Tropics. Once it cools in the upper atmosphere, the now-dry air descends, creating deserts in most areas it reaches, including the Atacama.

Second, the Atacama had some bad luck when it comes to ocean currents. The solid wall of South America forms a barrier. As a result, a major current hits the west coast of South America and flows like a river to the north. This current draws cold, dense water out of the Atacama Trench. Drawn to the surface, this cold flow of deep water does not evaporate easily. It generates low, dense coastal fogs when it hits the warm air, but little of that moisture rises up into the sky to create rain clouds. As a result, the cold current smothers the coastal rains that the west coast of Chile might otherwise expect. Fossil and geological evidence suggest that this cold, coastal current has dominated weather patterns in the Atacama for 150 million years.

Third, Atacama lies in the rain shadow of the Andes Mountains. Rainstorms and prevailing winds generated in the tropics on the other side of South America east of Brazil cannot get over the 20,000-foot-high (6,096 m) barrier of the Andes without being forced up so high that they lose their moisture as rain or snowfall.

DETECTING LIFE

When scientists wanted to test the robot destined to explore Mars, they took it to the driest, most lifeless place they could find, the Atacama Desert. They hoped that the austere desert could help solve a mystery and prevent a blunder.

Even before H. G. Wells wrote his terrifying *War of the Worlds*, scientists wondered if life had ever existed on Mars. They finally sent a Viking lander mission with instruments to analyze the soil in hopes of stirring up some biochemistry in their testing. What they found was a bizarre and unexpected chemical reaction, but they could not determine whether the reactions they recorded were caused by the last, faint traces of life in the Martian soil. So scientists resolved to build a more sensitive detector and try to solve the mystery of the odd chemistry of the Martian soil. The recent robotic rovers sent to Mars did find clear evidence that Mars once had liquid water, including floods, perhaps rivers and either small oceans or large lakes. However, the roving robots did not have instruments sensitive enough to determine whether Mars ever evolved at least microscopic organisms that left behind traces in the *amino acids* that living molecules manufacture.

So a team from the University of California at Berkeley designed instruments for a new Martian rover that could detect even the faintest trace of molecules associated with living cells. Then they sent the rover and its instrument package straight to the Atacama Desert, to search for life in a place where it had not rained in years and where the soil had no visible trace of topsoil, plants, or organic debris. Not only was the Atacama soil seemingly lifeless, it had the same red tint and some of the same unusual chemical properties as the Martian soils. If the instruments checked out there, they could fly on a 2011 European space mission. The instruments did find microscopic traces of amino acids in the desert soil, although at concentrations hundreds or thousands of times less than more temperate areas. The instruments even detected differences in the structures of the amino acids that proved conclusively they had been manufactured by living things. The scientists discovered they could safely redesign the instrument to make it even more sensitive, so that it can detect a trace of life 1,000 times more faint than the landers could pinpoint in the 1970s.

The team of geologists scoured the desert to find rocks that would give them some clue as to the climate that existed in the Atacama before it was a desert. They expected to find wet and dry periods, like the shifts that geologists have discovered in deserts like the Sahara. Instead, they found strong evidence that the Atacama has been locked in a desert climate with little relief for 150 million years. To their surprise, they found that the area was a desert long before continental shifts caused the Andes to begin rising some 30 million years ago, which means that the location on the globe and the cold, offshore current were more important factors than the rain shadow of the Andes.

A 22,000-YEAR RAINFALL RECORD

Desert conditions have seemingly always dominated, with only temporary periods that proved less harsh as a result of global climate changes. For instance, a recent report in *Science* presented a detailed account of rainfall in the Atacama going back 22,000 years. The researchers from the U.S. Geological Survey, the University of Arizona, and the Universidad de Chile analyzed pack rat nests and samples taken from dry lakebeds. Several Atacama rodents closely resemble the big-eyed, inquisitive pack rats of the American Southwest. Like their North American counterparts, the pack rats build nests from sticks, cactus, and debris, which their urine cements and preserves. As a result, scientists can analyze a pack rat *midden* and come up with a precise estimate of all the plants the rodent gathered up nearby when he lived there. This enables scientists to reconstruct rainfall patterns from the contents of the ancient nests, virtually fossilized by the urine of their makers.

In addition, the scientists analyzed layers of mineral deposits and sediment at a handful of springs, both those still active and those that dried up thousands of years ago. The flow of those springs affects the expansion and contraction of surrounding wetlands, which is reflected in the layers of ancient mud and the types of often-microscopic creatures that lived in the wetland. As a result, the springs can record fluctuations in rainfall.

The study demonstrated that although the Atacama has remained a hard-core desert all that time, global and local climate shifts did result in periods when the rain increased five- or 10-fold. For instance, between 16,000 and 10,000 years ago, rains increased and some desert areas shifted over to grasslands. Interestingly enough, the same thing was happening in areas of the Sahara Desert half a world away. During this period, higher elevation shrubs moved down off the mountains and out into what biologists today call the Absolute Desert, where virtually nothing grows.

The region dried out again 10,000 years ago and remained barren and waterless, except for one odd and unexplained period from 8,000 to about 3,000 years ago. During that time, the evidence from the springs suggested that rainfall had roughly tripled. However, the levels of dried lakes in the area did not change. So it is possible that the increased rainfall only hit the Andes, since runoff from the Andes feeds the springs in the Atacama.

The Atacama hides all sorts of odd little secrets, some of which have led to war and death. For instance, during the 19th century, the early explorers of this seemingly worthless region were astonished to find rich deposits of nitrates in the soil. Nitrates are vital in fertilizer, gunpowder, and plant growth, but at that time no one knew how to manufacture them. As a result, such natural sources of nitrates as bat and bird droppings were valuable. In the Atacama, the soil contained high concentrations of nitrates from some mysterious source.

The discovery triggered conflict among Chile, Bolivia, and Peru. When explorers discovered the nitrates, the area was controlled by Bolivia and Peru. However, the American-based mining companies extracting copper from Chile immediately saw the value of mining those nitrate deposits. One thing led to another and the three countries fought the War of the Pacific between 1879 and 1883. Chile won and laid claim to the area, a bitter bit of history that still riles Peru and Bolivia, which lost their access to the sea as a result of the defeat. Chile's economy depended heavily on mining the nitrate deposits until World War I, as the mining companies invaded the desert and extracted some 3 million tons per year. At one point, Chile had a near world monopoly on nitrate. However, the bonanza ended when other countries learned how to manufacture nitrate artificially.

Much later, scientists figured out where the nitrate came from. Turns out, the nitrates came from microscopic *plankton* living in the nearby ocean. Plankton use the sun's energy to take nitrogen out of the atmosphere and convert it into forms other creatures can use. When the microscopic plankton die, they sink down into the depths of the Atacama Trench. Eventually, winds blowing off the shore of Chile drive surface currents that cause upwelling and bring this deep, cold, nitrogen-rich water to the surface. That plankton-produced nitrogen then gets caught up in the fogs that form regularly along the coast. In the course of millions of years, winds have carried traces of that nitrogen-rich fog up and into the desert high in the Andes. Since the desert has existed for 150 million years, the soil never developed the rich layering of plants, bacteria, fungus, and other organisms that might use the nitrate, so it just accumulated.

As it turns out, the same trench and ocean currents that produced the nitrates have played a crucial role in creating the desert itself. The connection between the geography of the seafloor and the presence of the desert illustrates the importance of vast, global forces like the shifting of crustal plates in determining the boundary between deserts, forests, jungles, and grasslands. The roots of the world's oldest, driest desert go deep down into the Atacama Trench, which runs 100 miles (160 km) off the coast of South America for 3,666 miles (5,900 km). The trench is up to 26,460 feet deep (8,800 m) and 40 miles wide (65 km), with an area of 228,000 square miles (365,000 sq km).

EL NIÑO WREAKS HAVOC

The complex, interrelated geology of the Andes, the Atacama Desert, and the Atacama Trench all come together in the face of El Niño, a weather pattern that affects the whole planet. The microscopic plankton that grow in the sunlit waters of the upper ocean provide the foundation for the ocean's food chain, just as grass does on land. Some of the plankton that grow in the water near the surface sink to the bottom when they die. In shallow waters, a rich community of creatures lives on this rain of nutrients. But in deep, lightless places like the Atacama Trench, few bottom-dwelling creatures exist to harvest the drift of organic debris. So the nutrients accumulate in the trenches. Normally, prevailing winds blow down from the Andes across the Atacama Desert and on out to sea, which drives strong surface currents. These surface currents create an upwelling that brings nutrient-rich water up from deep in the Atacama Trench. This normally makes the seas off the coast of Chile heaven for fish, especially sardines and all the larger fish that eat them.

But every two to seven years, warm water sweeps in close to the coast, part of a global cycle in wind and ocean patterns. The warm water cuts off the nutrient-rich upwelling and devastates the fish, fishermen, sea birds, and sea lions, all of which are connected by the food chain. This warm surface current also generates a deluge of rainstorms, which batter the Andes and the coast of Chile.

This pattern of periodic warm surface currents off the coast of South America has been dubbed El Niño. The cycle has persisted already for thousands of years, as demonstrated by the way in which the Inca built their cities and irrigation canals. Clearly, they had adapted to these cycles of drought and flood.

No one is quite certain what triggers El Niño, but it apparently connects to the failure of the trade winds at the equator. Those trade winds, in turn, are directly connected to the atmospheric circulation that produces deserts along about 30 degrees of latitude in both the Northern and Southern Hemispheres. For some reason, these trade winds periodically weaken and then reverse themselves. This causes more storms in the Pacific and southern North America, but decreases storms and hurricanes in the Atlantic.

The effects can be devastating. One terrible El Niño event brought drought in India between 1789 and 1793 and caused an estimated 600,000 deaths due to starvation. El Niño increases the odds of wildfires throughout the world and droughts in Indonesia, Eastern Australia, New Guinea, West Africa, and northern South America. The 1982–1983 El Niño caused floods and *typhoons* that killed 2,000 people in the United States, Peru, Ecuador, Bolivia, Cuba, Hawaii, and Tahiti and brought drought elsewhere. Estimates put damages at a total of $13 billion.

The trench echoes the Andes Mountains, which tower to heights of up to 19,700 feet (6,600 m). That makes the rise from the bottom of the trench to the top of the Andes an altitude gain of 40,000 feet (1,300 m) in a width of 50 miles (80 km), the greatest such change in elevation on the planet. The Andes continue to rise at a faster rate than almost any other mountain range in the world as a result of the collision of two crustal plates along the line of the Atacama Trench and the connected East Pacific Rise. Here the Pacific Plate and the South American Plate collide, trapping between them the smaller Nazca Plate in the slow-motion geological train wreck. Along the line of the East Pacific Rise, the crust of the Earth is splitting apart at a rate of seven inches (178 mm) per year, the fastest such spreading rate on the planet. By contrast, the Atacama Trench formed where the small, dense, 3.8-mile-thick (6 km) Nazca plate was forced down under the lighter, 25-mile-thick (40 km) South American plate. The lurching of one plate under the other creates both the deep undersea trench and the awesome uplift of the Andes.

That slow-motion collision has also shaped the spectacular geology of Chile and Peru and the placement of the Atacama Desert. As the Nazca Plate descended into the Earth, it heated, melted, and fed volcanoes and frequent, devastating earthquakes. Seismologists plotting earthquake epicenters have concluded that the leading edge of the doomed Nazca Plate is breaking up some 500 miles (800 km) beneath the surface.

The two plates first collided as the supercontinent Pangaea was breaking up some 200 million years ago. The complex geology of the Andes bears witness to that geological history. The oldest, tilted rocks in its peaks date back 250 to 450 million years. But mostly the Andes are made of younger volcanoes. The Andes now have two, jagged, parallel lines of peaks separated by a high, flat valley.

Studies of the rocks and gases still spewing from those volcanoes have revealed remarkable connections to the deepest levels of Earth. Geologists suspect that the volcanic plumbing of the Andes goes clear down to Earth's mantle. Geologist David Lamb risked his life to take readings from scalding volcanic vents and discovered traces of helium direct from the Earth's mantle. Helium is a simple, almost indestructible element from which the fusion fires of stars have forged most of the more complex elements in the universe. So the forces that built the Andes connect back directly to the primordial stuff of the universe.

Recently, geologists Simon Lamb and Paul Davis came up with an intriguing theory to explain why the Andes are rising so quickly. They figured that the rise of the Andes must be controlled by what was happening down in the bottom of the Atacama Trench, where one plate was sliding under the other. They reasoned that the friction between those two plates should determine both the rise of the Andes and the region's sometimes devastating earthquakes. Usually, strain builds up on those buried pieces of crust until the strain overcomes the friction between the rocks of the two plates. The result is an earthquake that raises or lowers the mountains. But as the geologists studied earthquake measurements, they discovered that the largest earthquakes occurred directly opposite stretches of the Atacama Trench that had the most mud in the bottom. By contrast, the sections of the trench opposite the Atacama Desert in central and northern Chile generated much smaller earthquakes. Intrigued, they also compared the rate of mountain uplift to the sediment in the corresponding section of the trench. Once again, it fit.

Clearly, erosion from the continent washed mud down into the trench at greatly varying rates. In the south, several rivers rush down from the Andes and dump mud into the ocean. Here, the trench has nearly filled up with miles of mud. But in the north, in the desert areas, few rivers or streams reach the sea. Along this stretch of coast the trench plunges to five miles deep (8 km) with only a thin layer of sediment washed down from the mountains. Here, the mountains are also the highest and earthquakes most infrequent.

The geologists concluded that the sediment washed into the trench actually helped lubricate the boundary between the two plates, even miles beneath the surface.

Glossary

acidic   a substance that forms acids, which dissolve certain metals or reacts with bases or alkalis to form salts

amino acid   an organic compound with both an amino group and a carboxylic acid group that link together by peptide bonds to form proteins

Ancestral Puebloan   or Ancient Pueblo People, names for the pueblo-building groups who lived in the American Southwest until about 1400, often known as the Anasazi

archaeologist   a scientist who studies the past by examining the remains of past civilizations

arroyo   a Spanish term for a usually dry wash or river channel in an arid region

basalt   a hard, dense, dark volcanic rock composed chiefly of plagioclase, pyroxene, and olivine, often having a glassy appearance

basin and range   the alternation of mountain chains and intervening low valleys or basins that dominates the geography of the American Southwest

bedouin   a desert-dwelling Arab of the Arabian or North African deserts

borax   a hydrated sodium borate, an ore of boron, used as a cleaning compound

carbohydrates   a group of organic compounds that includes sugars, starches, celluloses, and gums that serves as a major energy source for animals

catacombs   underground burial caves

Cenozoic   the most recent era of geologic time, including the Tertiary and Quaternary periods during which continents took their current form

chlorophyll   green pigments found in photosynthetic organisms

Colorado squawfish   a now-endangered fish that reached lengths of more than six feet that lived in the flood-prone Colorado River

continental drift   the theory that invokes currents deep in the Earth and a series of volcanic ridges and trenches to account for the movement of continents

cycads   palmlike cone-bearing evergreen plants of the division Cycadophyta, native to warm areas that have large pinnately compound leaves

dehydration   removing water from a compound or organism

diatoms microscopic one-celled algae of the class *Bacillariophyceae* that have cell walls of silica

DNA a nucleic acid that codes a cell's genetic information and which makes copies of itself with the use of RNA; it has two chains of nucleotides twisted into a double helix and joined by hydrogen bonds

ecology the study of the relationships between living things and their environments

ecosystem a living community plus its environment, which functions as a unit

erosion the process of being eroded, or removed, usually from rainfall runoff

evaporate to change into a vapor

evolution the gradual change of species over time as a result of genetic mutations that increase their fitness as measured by the number of surviving offspring that reproduce and pass along the mutation; ultimately the source of the vast diversity of life; all contemporary organisms are related to each other through common descent

fungal hyphae rootlets from fungi that grow underground that often hold the soil together and frequently help other plant roots absorb moisture and nutrients

germination the sprouting of a seed

glaciologist a scientist who studies glaciers

gneiss a banded metamorphic rock, usually of the same composition as granite

graben a valley formed by the dropping of a piece of land between two fault lines

gypsum a common colorless, white, or yellowish mineral used in the manufacture of plaster of Paris, various plaster products, and fertilizers

hominids a primate of the family *Hominidae* that once had many species but which now consists of only *Homo sapiens*

hoodoos pillarlike rock formations, usually volcanic

hydrate to supply water to restore or maintain fluid balance

hydrocarbons organic compounds, such as benzene and methane, that contain only carbon and hydrogen

hypothalamus the part of the brain below the thalamus that regulates bodily temperature, some metabolic processes, and other autonomic activities

isotope the form of an atom that has the same number of neutrons and protons in the nucleus but fewer electrons

keystone species a species whose activity affects the entire ecosystem, such as a beaver

krypton an inert gaseous element used chiefly in fluorescent lamps

labyrinth a mazelike structure

lichens a fungus that grows cooperatively with algae and together forms a composite organism that forms a crustlike covering on rocks

lithium   a soft, highly reactive metallic element used as a heat transfer medium, in thermonuclear weapons, ceramics, glass, and even as a medication

loess   windblown (aeolian) soil

magma   the molten rock material under the Earth's crust, from which igneous rock forms

manganese   a silvery brittle metallic element found worldwide, especially in the ores pyrolusite and rhodochrosite and in nodules on the ocean floor used as an alloy to strengthen other metals

mantle   the semimolten layer of Earth between the crust and the core

marsupials   a group of mammal-like animals, i.e., the kangaroo, that sustain their helpless young in a pouch instead of in a womb

mastodons   giant, elephantlike creatures that died out at the end of the last Ice Age some 10,000 years ago

Mesozoic   the geologic age of the dinosaurs that lasted from 240 to 65 million years ago

metabolism   the physical and chemical processes by which a cell produces the elements necessary to live by breaking down some substances to produce energy and manufactures other substances

midden   the nest of a pack rat or other rodent

millennium   a thousand years

mitochondrial   relating to a spherical or elongated organelle inside nearly all eukaryotic cells that contains genetic material and enzymes crucial for cell metabolism and energy production

monocotyledons   plants that branch haphazardly

Neanderthals   an extinct species of the Homo genus that lived during the last Ice Age in Europe

plankton   microscopic organisms, including algae and protozoans, that drift in great numbers near the surface of fresh- or salt water and serve as the base of the food chain in the oceans

pollinators   insects, bats, and birds that assist in plant reproduction by spreading pollen from flower to flower

Precambrian   relating to the geologic Cambrian Period, the longest stretch of geologic history that includes the whole stretch of Earth's history before the emergence of complex, multicelled organisms some 500 million years ago; divided into the Archeozoic and Proterozoic eras

quartz   a very hard mineral composed of silica found worldwide in many different types of rocks, including sandstone and granite

rain shadow desert   a desert created by tall mountain ranges that block the flow of moisture-laden clouds

rhyolite   a fine-grained extrusive volcanic rock, similar to granite in composition and usually exhibiting flow lines

rift system   a volcanic system characterized by deep, narrow valleys or basins usual along the edge of a crustal plate

sedimentary   layers of dirt, sand, or other fine material laid down in layers by wind or water

semiarid   characterized by annual rainfall of 10 to 20 inches (25 to 50 cm) and having scrubby vegetation with short, coarse grasses

shale   a rock composed of layers of claylike, fine-grained sediments

summer solstice   the longest day of the year

theropod dinosaurs   carnivorous dinosaurs of the Jurassic and Cretaceous periods, characterized by short forelimbs

typhoons   a tropical cyclone occurring in the western Pacific or Indian oceans

Books

Abbey, Edward. *Beyond the Hill.* New York: Holt, Rinehart & Winston, 1984. Poetic examination of the soul of the desert by the writer who helped redefine images of the North American deserts in the popular mind.

Alcock, John. *Sonoran Desert Spring.* Tucson, Ariz.: University of Arizona Press, 1994. Excellent account of desert ecosystems and unique creatures by a biologist with an easy and accessible writing style.

Bagnold, Ralph A. *The Physics of Blown Sand and Desert Dunes.* London: Methuen & Co., 1941. Precise, sometimes lyrical description of the forces that shape sand dunes.

Bender, Gordon L., ed. *Reference Handbook on the Deserts of North America.* Westport, Conn.: Greenwood Press, 1982. Massive tome on the desert, presented through a series of usually readable, sometimes technical, essays.

Bowden, Charles. *Blue Desert.* Tucson, Ariz.: University of Arizona Press, Tucson, 1986. Beautifully written meditation on the Sonoran Desert near Tucson.

Brown, G. W., Jr. *Desert Biology.* Vols. 1. and 2. New York: Academic Press, 1965, 1974. Great resource and information, but sometimes technical series of essays on the worlds' deserts.

Cook, Ronald U., and Andrew Warren. *Geomorphology in Deserts.* Berkeley and Los Angeles: University of California Press, 1973. Definitive, usually readable account of how geography and climate combine to produce deserts.

George, Uwe. *The Deserts of This Earth.* New York: Harcourt Brace Jovanovich, 1977. Easy-to-read, general information.

Goetzmann, William H. *Exploration and Empire.* New York: Alfred A. Knopf, 1966. Great account of how deserts have shaped exploration and the history of North America.

Hornaday, William T. *Camp-fires on Desert and Lava.* New York: Charles Scribner's Sons, 1914. Entertaining adventures in Mexico's harsh, lava-strewn core of the Sonoran Desert.

Ingram, D. L., and L. E. Mount. *Man and Animals in Hot Environments.* New York: Springer-Verlag, 1975. Presents research on how to survive in desert heat and how animals have adapted to high temperatures.

Mabbutt, J. A. *Desert Landforms*. Cambridge, Mass.: MIT Press, 1977. Great, but technical, discussion of all desert landforms.

Macmahon, James. *Deserts*. New York: Alfred A. Knopf, 1985. Concisely written, beautifully illustrated, this definitive book contains an invaluable distillation of desert research.

Maloiy, G. M. O. *Comparative Physiology of Desert Animals*. New York: Academic Press, 1972. Easier to read than its title suggests.

McGinnies, William. *Discovering the Desert*. Tucson, Ariz.: University of Arizona Press, 1981. A strongly researched, scholarly book by one of the top experts on the desert.

Nabhan, Gary Paul. *Gathering the Desert*. Tucson, AZ.: University of Arizona Press, 1985. An expert on the use of desert plants by native peoples, Nabhan writes a sometimes poetic book about the way in which the desert has shaped fascinating and complex cultures.

Trimble, Stephen. *The Sagebrush Ocean: A Natural History of the Great Basin*. Reno, Nev.: University of Nevada Press, 1989. A beautifully illustrated book in a natural history series.

Wells, Stephen G., and Donald R. Haragan. *Origin and Evolution of Deserts*. Albuquerque, N.Mex.: University of New Mexico Press, 1983. Detailed essays on desert ecosystems.

Zwinger, Ann Haymond. *The Mysterious Lands*. New York: Truman Tallye Books/Plume, 1990. Scientifically solid, sometimes lyrical examination of the ecology of the deserts of North America.

Web Sites

Arizona Highways
http://www.arizonahighways.com
This international travel magazine posts frequent articles and images about the desert, usually the Sonoran, but sometimes the Mojave and Great Basin.

Desert USA
http://www.desertusa.com/glossary.html
This informative site is mostly geared toward providing useful facts and figures for anyone planning a visit to a North American desert.

geology.com
http://geology.com/news/2006/11/dust-from-sahara-and-gobi-deserts.html
This site provided by Google collects many images and scientific reports on geology topics, including many interesting postings on deserts of the world.

National Geographic
http://www.nationalgeographic.com/geographyaction/habitats/deserts_tundra.html
A search on this excellent, highly visual Web site will yield many interesting articles and images that relate to the world's deserts.

Scienceresearch.com
http://www.scienceresearch.com/search
A word search on this site that connects to a great mass of recently published scientific research will yield many interesting studies on the world's deserts.

United States Geological Survey
http://pubs.usgs.gov/gip/deserts
and http://www.usgs.gov/science/science.php?term=245
This wonderfully detailed, image-rich Web site provides a wealth of information about almost any geology topic, including many articles, images, and research results concerning the four North American deserts.

Wikipedia: Deserts
http://en.wikipedia.org/wiki/List_of_deserts
Good source for overview information about the world's deserts.

World Atlas of Panoramic Aerial Images
http://130.166.124.2/world_atlas/6/6.html
This site offers satellite images of the whole world, including the planet's major desert areas.

World Deserts: The Living Desert
http://www.livingdesert.org/deserts/world_deserts.asp
Interesting information about desert plants and animals provided by a desert preserve based in Palm Springs, California.

Index